Everybody's Prayerbook

❧ Finding God in My Life ❧

Edmund Flood

Sheed & Ward

Editorial Acknowledgements

I acknowledge with gratitude the co-editors of *Everybody's Prayerbook*: Alex Adkins (Anglican), Brenda Forward and Ernest Forward (Baptist), and David Butler (Methodist). Their collaboration has made possible an *ecumenical* prayerbook.

Copyright© 1991
Edmund Flood

Sheed & Ward™ is a service of National Catholic Reporter Publishing Company, Inc.

Library of Congress Catalog Card Number: 90-64029

ISBN: 1-55612-418-X

Published by: Sheed & Ward
                 115 E. Armour Blvd. P.O. Box 419492
                 Kansas City, MO 64141-6492

To order, call: (800) 333-7373

Contents

Finding God in My Life
  Why Pray? 1
  How to Use This Book for Prayer 1

Your Home
  Do You Feel At Home 3
  The Strong Deep River 5

Doing Jobs Around the Home
  Hotel? Orchestra? or Jazz Band? 7
  *Not **What** You Do, but **How*** 9

Shared Activities
  Holidays Together 11
  Discovering the Other 13

Meals
  Christian-type Meals 15
  Our Meals: Their Enemies and Friends 17

Holidays and Relaxation
  Discovering Each Other 19
  Overcoming the Obstacles 21

Disagreements and Anger
  Are Disagreements OK? 23
  Two Cheers for My Anger 25

Sexuality
  Thank God for My Sexuality 27
  Riding the Troughs 29

My Close Relationships
  True Love 31
  Someone You Love Deeply 33

Dependents
  Children 35
  The Elderly 37

Good Friends
  Good Friends: How Important? 39
  Born for Friendship? 41

The Weekend
    The Opportunities 43
    Sunday 45

My Neighbors
    Who Needs Neighbors? 47
    Gateways to Good News 49

Our Neighborhood
    What's Your Neighborhood to You? 51
    Neighborliness in Practice 53

My Decisions
    How Important? 55
    Finding the Way 57

Money
    The Plus Side? 59
    The Minus Side? 61

Good Times
    Appreciation 63
    The Difference Looking Makes 65

Bad Times
    How Bad? 67
    Our Suffering and Jesus 69

Our World—and our Grandchildren
    "A New Groundswell" 71
    Who Will Save Our Grandchildren a World? 73

Your Job
    Your Job: Good or Bad? 75
    Making Work Good 77

The People I Work With
    The Bond of Respect 79
    The Bond of Shared Experience 81

Your Boss
    Problems? 83
    Towards Solutions 85

My Faith
    What Difference Does It Make? 87
    All Shall Be Well 89

My Church
    What's My Church To Me? 91
    What's My Church To Them? 93

Our Worship
    Enjoy 95
    Expressing Who We Are 97

Death
    Death: How Bad? 99
    We Shall Not Die Alone 101

Fullness of Life
    How Different From This One? 103
    What Will It Feel Like? 105

Acknowledgements

The Scripture quotations used in this publication are from the *Good News Bible*, published by the Bible Societies and Collins. Old Testament: ©American Bible Society, New York 1976. New Testament: ©American Bible Society, New York 1966, 1971, and 4th edition 1976. Used by permission.

The Strong Deep River: Dolores Curran, *Traits of a healthy family*, Minnesota, 1983.

Our Meals: Their Enemies and Friends: Dolores Curran (as above).

Discovering Each Other: Ann McCarroll, "Getting to know children requires lots of good talk," Christian Science Monitor News Service, and *Denver Post*, June 11, 1980.

Overcoming the Obstacles: John Haughey, *Converting 9 to 5*, New York, 1989.

Are Disagreements OK?: Dolores Curran, as above.

True Love: Morton T. Kelsey, *Caring: how we love one another*, New York, 1981.

Children: Morton T. Kelsey, as above.

Born for Friendship?: Andrew Greeley, *The Friendship Game*, New York, 1970.

Gateways to Good News: Dolores Curran, as above.

The Minus Side?: Morton T. Kelsey, as above.

The Difference Looking Makes: Gerard Manley Hopkins, "God's Grandeur," *Poems*, London, 1953.

How Bad?: Dolores Curran, as above; John Macquarrie, *In Search of Humanity*, London, 1982.

"A New Groundswell": Hubert H. Humphrey, Insititute of Public Affairs.

Your Job: Good or Bad?: Henley Forecasting Center in Britain.

Making Work Good: John Naisbitt, *Re-inventing the Corporation*, London, 1986.

The Bond of Respect: John Haughey, as above.

The Bond of Shared Experience: The two stages: John Haughey, as above.

Problems?: Warren Bennis & Burt Nanus, *Leaders: the strategies of taking charge*, San Francisco, 1985; Charles Handy, *The Age of Unreason*, London, 1989; Robert Levering, et al., *The 100 Best Companies to Work for in America*, Addison-Wesley, 1984; Tad Tuleja, *Beyond the Bottom Line*, Oxford, 1985; *Harvard Business Review*, 1989.

Towards Solutions: Charles Handy, as above.

All Shall Be Well: Gerhard von Rad, *Old Testament Theology*, Edinburgh, 1962; David E. Jenkins, *God, Jesus and Life in the Spirit*, London, 1988.

What's My Church to Them?: Diarmuid O'Murchu MSC NACCAN; *Faith in the City* (Archbishop of Canterbury's Commission on Urban Priority Areas), London, 1985.

Enjoy: Harvey H. Guthrie, *Theology as Thanksgiving*, New York, 1981.

Expressing Who We Are: David Morland, *Eucharist and Justice*, London, 1971; Allen, *The Framework is Covenant*; Mary Grey, *In Search of the Sacred*.

Death: How Bad?: K. Rahner, *Theological Investigations*, XIX, London, 1984.

What Will It *Feel* Life?: Hans Küng, *Eternal Life?*, London, 1984; Brian Hebblethwaite, *The Christian Hope*, Basingstoke, 1984.

Finding God in My Life

Why Pray?

We know that our job is to be human. In the people we know, and in our own relationships, we have learned a lot about what that job means.

Through Jesus, God showed himself to be at the center of our quest to be human. I get together a quick snack, or prepare a meal, for someone I love; I work a long day at the office or the factory. In all the many kinds of activities I'm involved in each day, God and I are in partnership so far as I try to make my "patch" more human. Through me God's "Kingdom" or Rule is coming, as Jesus showed us, to transform our world. No wonder we call that "being creative"!

The chief adventure of a Christian's life is the discovery of all that means. I discover the significance of *God* being partner in my own story. My partner is characterized by love and faithfulness, who brings life out of death. Through Jesus he showed how deeply he cares for all, like a mother or a shepherd.

Our prayer is where we open our eyes and hearts to this discovery of God at the center of all we do. It's where we get in touch with our true selves. We turn to some part of our experience and give it the space to unfold.

How to Use This Book for Prayer

This book is designed to help you focus on experiences that most of us have. You can do that at any time, and in any way you choose: you know what best suits you.

You could use it over a year, exploring a new topic each fortnight. There are two or three steps or sections in each topic. By taking one at a time, over that fortnight, you may find you are giving yourself the best chance to explore that area quite fully. You may, on the other hand, feel it best to give less time to each topic.

1

Experience

Each section starts with your experience of that area of your life.

Reflection

It then leads you into reflecting on your experience: with the help of Jesus entering into its deeper significance and direction, so as to find your Father and Partner there, guiding you to become more like Christ for the world he loves.

Response

Each section ends with a Response to what you have become more aware of, whether a prayer or a commitment to some action.

Both this Reflection and this Response are what we call "Prayer."

Allocate a few days to each section. Do your best to find regular times when you can relax (ideally with some music), and give all your attention to this section, and eventually the topic as a whole.

Even if you can't find regular times to pray, grab some minutes in traffic jams, or the bus or the train, or wherever, to reflect on that area of your life and on all it can show.

Your Home

❧ Do You Feel at Home? ❧

Experience

Where you live can be just a convenient shelter. But what most of us want is to live in a place where we feel deeply at home.

What can give us this feeling?

It's partly a matter of possession: this place is mine.

Then there's the feeling of being valued and wanted. When I'm absent I'm missed. My presence brings pleasure. I'm loved for who I am.

What are your most valued experiences of feeling at home? What especially contributed to them?

Reflection

For some periods of our lives, we have that kind of experience. If we have at some stage lacked it, it can mean even more to us.

Sometimes we are conscious of its vulnerability. It is vulnerable to disagreements and misunderstandings. Even when it is strong, we may take it for granted and not appreciate it enough. And we know that we and the others who make up this home will one day be parted.

But if we are able to find God in our lives, this situation is transformed.

First, "everything belongs to you: this world, life and death, the present and the future" (1 Cor. 3:21-22). Whatever happens to me, wherever I go is mine, because I am a partner of God in his work of human transformation.

Jesus' Good News was that God's "Kingdom," or creative power, is now alive in our world. He is making the life of our world more human. He calls us to own this world and feel at home in it, by sharing lovingly in his work.

Response

If I'm really sharing in God's work, I will not only enjoy this consciousness but also want it for others: particularly those close to me, in my home.

Like God, I want them to feel that all I have is theirs; that they are valued and wanted; that they are loved for who they are, and that their presence brings pleasure.

Spend some minutes listening to what Jesus is saying to you about *his desire that you and everyone feel at home everywhere and always*. Your listening may be helped by:

• your imagining yourself at one of Jesus' meals in the house he used at Capernaum: how did he treat his disciples, the prostitutes, the Pharisees?

• your listening to him describing the father's welcome home of the prodigal son:

> The son was still a long way from home when his father saw him; his heart was filled with compassion, and he ran, threw his arms round his son, and kissed him.
>
> "Hurry!" he said. "Bring the best robe and put it on him. Go and get the prize calf and kill it, and let us celebrate with a feast" (Luke 15:20-23).

ஃ The Strong Deep River ஃ

Experience

"Without communication, you don't know one another. If you don't know one another, you don't care about one another, and that's what the family ballgame is all about."

When is communication in your home at its best?

What helps to make it so?

What have you learned from the successes—and the failures?

Reflection

When you think of families you know well, you realize that each has problems in their relationships. One member is warm and outgoing; another is reserved. One likes a relaxed and casual kind of life; another prefers a well-structured existence. As a result, everyday situations are quite often being approached from different angles, different needs, and different feelings. When the matter is important, or when people feel down, the differences can cause pain.

How do you handle such differences at home?

There will be rows. Under pressure, we can express our resentment or anger sharply.

But if we're mature, what will really count is that there is a strong, deep river of knowing and caring for each other running below the temporary turbulences.

Many don't bother much about creating that river. They make little effort to share thoughts and feelings. "Passivity and silence on the part of husbands are most often mentioned by wives as the major problem with their marriage."

5

But, as a Christian, I know I shall be judged by what I have tried to do in "the tough labor of love" (1 Thessal. 1:3). "Love builds up," Paul also said (1 Cor. 8:1). Gradually, and often with difficulty, I get to know the feelings, the strengths and weaknesses, of those in my home. So far as I am able, I get to see and feel things as they do, so that I can give them the support and love they need.

Because I'm no longer seeing myself as the center of the universe, I'm now able to find God. God is not found in self-centeredness, in words and theories, but only in our labor of love: in our creating that strong, deep river of knowing and caring for each other.

Response

Thank God for the fact that he is found in the very center of our lives:

- when we're really trying to know and care
- when we're encouraging and supporting good in others
- when we're making them feel wanted and at home

Sit for some minutes and let this God at the heart of your life speak to you about his own love for you, and about what he wants for you.

Doing Jobs Around the Home

❧ Hotel? Orchestra? or Jazz Band? ❧

Experience

Bill most enjoys doing structural jobs around the home, then computers, then talk with the family.

Nan most likes talk with the family, then gardening, then certain kinds of cooking.

Their three children are equally different!

How ordinary that sounds! But I know from many visits that that home has special qualities of relaxedness, humor and joy.

This comes from the fact that *each* of them takes obvious pleasure and pride in their *different* enthusiasms, tastes and roles. They sometimes laugh at each other's enthusiasms, but it's a laughter of enjoyment, not of derision.

That family *could* have been like a Hotel: each doing their own job like a machine, and just taken for granted.

It could have been like an Orchestra: with the contribution of each enjoyed, but limited to a preset score.

Instead, the family is like a Jazz Band. Each enjoys "playing" like his or her own self, as a member of this family, and "owns" and enjoys the others also doing so.

When you consider the jobs being done by yourself and others around the home, which of these three models is preponderant?

Reflection

Bill and Nan don't happen to be aware of any close connection between what they have created and Christianity.

Yet the Scripture ideal of *any* Christian community is similar to theirs.

It's not meant to be just an efficient machine or just to follow a preset score. The primary reality is each person's gifts and character, to be respected, "owned" and enjoyed, as that person uses it for the service of others.

It's in those gifts ("charisms") that we all can experience God's loving-kindness ("charis") and "energy" (1 Cor. 12:4-7).

A list of possible gifts tumbles off Paul's pages. There's no preset list; and the role of the conductor gets no emphasis.

All the emphasis is on the joy of finding God's kindness and energy in each other's *different* roles and characters and on our responding to them accordingly.

For a family to live successfully mainly *by the jazz band model, what degree of maturity would it need to have?*

Response

Quietly, unobtrusively, through non-Christians and Christians, God is always leading us on to find him in a fuller kind of life.

Reflect on your own experience of that in your home setting or elsewhere as you say:

> *Praise the Lord with trumpets,*
> *praise him with harps and lyres,*
> *praise him with drums and dancing,*
> *with harps and flutes and cymbals.*

> *Praise the Lord, all living creatures (Psalm 150).*

⮾ Not *What* You Do, but *How* ⮾

Experience

Jack comes home one night, tired and discouraged. No one's at home. There's a note on the kitchen table: "Your dinner's in the dog"!

A caricature, of course. But would it *feel* so far from the truth to someone who comes home late at night from a stressful meeting, if he or she found everyone gone to bed, and no snack or note of greeting?

How different to find a little meal left out, and an affectionate note!

We know that "it's the thought that counts." It is important *how we divide the labor.* Still more important, though, is *how we treat our fellow-laborers.*

How is appreciation, encouragement and support shown in your home?

Reflection

St. Paul's letters give us the profoundest picture we have of what a Christian community should be.

Love, we know, is the center. But for Paul that isn't just a nice feeling for when things are going smoothly: it's "building up" the other person.

The Christians at Corinth led him a real dance. But even to them he could write that "everything we do, dear friends, is to build you up" (2 Cor. 12:19).

The Thessalonians were his hope and joy. "We were gentle when we were with you, like a mother taking care of her children, because of our love for you. We were ready to share with you not only the Good News from God but even our own lives. You were so dear to us!" (1 Thess. 2:7-8)

Reflect on that relationship, and also on people you know in your home and elsewhere who try to flesh out in their lives the only Christian "Law."

What difference can that "Law" make in practice? God made it the one requirement for a fruitful life: does your own experience prompt you to see that as an imposition to be resented or as something very different?

Response

1. Who does most of the chores in your home?

List a few ways in which appreciation, encouragement and support have been shown recently in your home to him or her:

_____

_____

_____

_____

_____

_____

2. Take the list you've just made, and share with God your feelings about what is already being done to "build up" people in your home, and the difference it makes.

Share also with God your feelings about what more needs to be done, and what more *you* will do, to become more like Christ in your home.

Shared Activities

❧ Holidays Together ❧

Experience

You have a beautiful picture in your home, but in the rush of everyday life you hardly notice it. It's equally easy to fail to appreciate a view or a building we regularly pass. It's even true of a person we're often with.

Really to appreciate even just physical things we have to stand back, relax, and focus our mind and feelings on them. Only in that way, normally, can their special qualities shine out for us and stir us.

Since human beings are more complex and have greater depth, they obviously have even less chance of really becoming known to us unless we relax with them enough to look closely and so enjoy what we can then see in them.

How far have some of your holidays helped you to better appreciate and enjoy close friends? In what ways did they do that?

Reflection

Christianity is often thought of as doleful and against human pleasures, like sex. But in fact its basic mindset is the very reverse.

Just as the climax of God's act of creation was to "rest" and see that it is good, so all is not ours, as God intends, until we "rest" and see how good it is.

A relaxed sense of wonder and thanks for people and events was the hallmark of Jesus' way. His suppers and his stories showed that. It lies at the heart of the Eucharist.

On our holidays we can take up activities (including perhaps sleep!) for which we usually have too little time. We hope the holiday will refresh

11

us. But their best contribution may be as a means to open our eyes more fully to the qualities and even splendor in the people we thought we knew well but have only imperfectly discovered. Is this kind of "rest" important to you on your holidays?

Response

O Lord, our Lord, your greatness is seen in all the world!

When I look at the sky, which you have made,
    at the moon and the stars, which you set in their place—
What is man and woman, that you think of them;
    mere men and women, that you care for them?

Yet you made them inferior only to yourself;
    you crowned them with glory and honor.
You appointed them rulers over everything you made,
    you placed them over all creation.

O Lord, our Lord,
    your greatness is seen in all the world! (Psalm 8)

ᨠ Discovering the Other ᨠ

Experience

Which shared activities mean a lot to you?

Of course, they can interest you for purely selfish reasons. You're good at a game; and you need someone to play with or an audience.

But they can also be an ideal way to discover another person. I went to the theater last week with my sister. I greatly enjoyed the play; but my enjoyment was increased even further by seeing her enjoyment. In the interval and at supper afterwards we discovered other shared tastes and interests.

The sharing can help us discover and enjoy what makes the other "tick": what makes him or her this special person.

It's not a discovery just of information, as you might get from a questionnaire; but a discovery through openness to the other's experience, values and feelings.

Have some of your shared activities led you to that kind of discovery?

If so, how important are they to you?

Reflection

All men and women were made to love, and to be loved. But is it really love until you "get inside" the other's personality: their experience, values and feelings? And don't these come to expression less in discussion than in action?

In the rush of modern living, opportunities for this can be rare. Recognizing this, "most contented families tend to share at least one leisure activity weekly." They find that, without some such strategy, the opportunities will vanish, perhaps for months.

Of course there are many other strategies that families adopt, according to their circumstances. They may try to make preparing a meal, and clearing up afterwards, a more shared kind of activity. Children are given responsibility for some household tasks—often with excellent results both for family life and for their own development. Or a family doesn't just have its collective times together, but also encourages shared activities *in pairs*, especially the husband and wife.

As we sort out the strategies that suit us best, we realize increasingly that the love "command" is, in a way, wrongly so called. It's not a restriction, an imposition, but *a guide to truly human life.*

It's not encouraging us to "love" the other as a mere object out there, but to learn to know, enjoy, and share with that person in their special dynamism and outlook.

Response

> Jesus, my brother and Lord,
> > the Gospel stories give me a glimpse of your learning to know,
> > enjoy and share in the special dynamism of the people
> > who came to you:
> > the fishing trips, the stories, the journeys,
> > and especially the meals.
>
> "Here is the summit of God's creation," you say to us:
> > "each with their own special dynamism and outlook.
>
> By sharing deeply with them you'll share what I found:
> > that in ordinary, imperfect human beings
> > we can enjoy and be involved in
> > the vibrancy and the checkered splendor of God."

Meals

❧ Christian-type Meals ❧

Experience

On the way to work most of us grab some things from the fridge or skip breakfast altogether. Lunch may be as rapid. Only in the evenings and on the weekends may relaxed meals together be possible. With different working patterns and TV, they may be infrequent even then.

Even so, most of us succeed in having a relaxed meal together either regularly or occasionally.

Think of occasions when you enjoyed relaxed meals. What would you have lost if you hadn't had them?

Reflection

Scripture can help us to appreciate what a family meal can be for a Christian:

• it can increase our sense of *loyalty to those present* (as Orientals, Jesus and the Jews believed this strongly)

• the enjoyment of food and drink helps us to realize *the goodness of creation* and *the goodness of enjoying it together*. The prayers at table can reinforce that.

• a family meal in a full sense is not just for eating, but may also be *our main way of meeting*. In Paul's churches, eating and meeting spilled into each other. Paul indicates some central characteristics of those occasions:

   • you *TOOK EACH OTHER'S GIFTS SERIOUSLY,* as manifestations of God's practical kindness and transforming power deeply present in our lives (1 Cor. 12:4-7).

15

- you *LISTENED TO EACH OTHER*, even when you yourself believed you had an important thing to say (1 Cor. 14:30).

- you *HONORED EACH OTHER*.

- you *TOOK PLEASURE IN EACH OTHER'S SUCCESSES AND SHOWED SYMPATHY FOR EACH OTHER'S FAILURES OR MISFORTUNES* (12:26).

For Paul, Christian life without that kind of regular communication between the members of a community or family was inconceivable. How seriously should we take that view?

Response

1. "The Word became Flesh and dwelt among us" (literally: came to live in our street).

Reflect on how merrily and wholeheartedly the Word embraces our humanity and invites us to join him in that.*

Decide on any ways in which you could use meals more fully as an opportunity for this.

2. *Lord Jesus, meals were so often your signature tune.*

> *How often, far into the night,*
> *in that little Capernaum house and its shared courtyard, people*
> *could hear the laughter and see the happiness*
> *you brought to all around that table.*

> *Help us recognize you, Lord Jesus,*
> *in our 'breaking of bread,'*
> *where we share not just food*
> *but ourselves.*

*For details of Jesus' meals and of his life, see my book *The Jesus Story*, (Sheed & Ward, 1991).

16

֍ Our Meals: Their Enemies and Friends ֍

Experience

Enemies of Meals

Enemies to the Christian quality of our meals come in many forms.

"Many families see nothing wrong with turning the family table over to TV viewing: so there is slim hope for a daily period of sharing, caring and feeling."

"In many families the table becomes a place on which to dump the day's frustrations, invectives on one another, silence."

What are the main enemies to your meals?

Friends of Meals

We all know of possible helps toward our achieving a Christian quality to our meals. Here is a short list to which you can add in the space beneath:

1. Appreciation and help for the person who cooks this meal;

2. Really wanting everyone there to enjoy the food and being together;

3. Being sensitive to people's present emotional needs: someone at the table may have had a bad day, or a very good day, for example;

4. Listening to people: not just words, but also feelings;

5. Hospitality, both to friends, and to those particularly in need of it.

6._____

_____

7._____

_____

Reflection

Reflect on recent experiences you have had of any "enemies" or "friends" to the Christian quality of your meals and on any conclusions you may draw from this experience.

Response

> Listen! I stand at the door and knock;
>   if anyone hears my voice and opens the door,
> I will come into that person's house and eat with him or her,
>   and he or she will eat with me (Revelation 3:20).

Respond to this invitation in your own way.

We are called to enjoy a life of intimate sharing, support and loyalty.

Recall some of your best experiences of meals in the light of this.

As you do so, you could invite more fully into your life the one who stands at your door and knocks.

Holidays and Relaxation

❧ Discovering Each Other ❧

Experience

This family had long shared holidays and outings together. John, a teenager, said in an interview:

"The best time I have had with my dad was when burglars broke into our summer cottage at the lake. The police said we should come up to see what was missing. Well, our family's made the trip dozens of times, but this time there were just the two of us. It's a six hour drive. Six hours up, six hours back. No car radio. We really talked. It's like we discovered each other. There's more to him than I thought. It made us friends."

"It's like we discovered each other." That hadn't happened on those regular holidays and outings. We know it can. What makes it happen for you/others?

Reflection

RELAXATION today is very necessary. We do need to "recharge our batteries."

It can be people with separate trays in front of a TV set or it can be people relaxing and communicating in a living room or a garden, or round a table, or where you will. Perhaps most of us need both?

HOLIDAYS can be where the presence of others has no great significance for our enjoyment, or it can include getting to know one another better. John reminds us that the second option can elude us if we don't make it our definite aim.

Reflect on times of relaxation or holidays when you have come to know someone with you much better and felt really at one with them.

The Jewish greeting today is the same as in Jesus' time: "Shalom." It wishes on you "peace" not just as an absence of strife but a state of oneness and wholeness as a man or woman.

Oneness with those we love is a deep yearning in all of us. It's a part of our feeling of being at home—of being our true selves—in God's creation.

Response

1. Thank God for the opportunities you have for this.

2. Are there people close to you who particularly need such opportunities to be created? What difference would it be likely to make to them? Can you help?

3. "Peace is what I leave you; it is my own peace that I give to you" (John 14:27).

Thank God, in your own way, for times of relaxation, peace, oneness and wholeness that you have experienced, and for what these say to you about God and his purpose for you.

As you do so, you could say, from time to time:

"May God, our source of peace, be with us all" (Romans 15:33).

❧ Overcoming the Obstacles ❧

Experience

In the 1950s my uncle always got back from work to his home in the suburbs by 4:30 so as to have tea with his young daughter. Which of us could even think of doing that today?

The pace of modern life isn't the only barrier to our discovering each other. Some of the obstacles arise from aspects of modern life that can quite largely be welcomed, like TV, and our recognizing that the 'teens are a training for independence, when peer contact is fruitful and necessary.

A more serious obstacle is the media's idea that *fun consists mainly in engaging in expensive activities.* That can lead us to feel that enjoying such activity, not people, is what people mainly want from holidays and time off.

What are your own set of opportunities and obstacles to relaxing together?

To what extent is the humanness of your environment at stake here?

Reflection

Reflect on *the most human moments in your life.* Some of them are likely to have been at times of holidays or relaxation.

Paul describes our life in Christ as when "we have kindness and compassion for one another, have the same thoughts, share the same love, and look out for one another's interests" (Philippians 2:1-4).

That was the attitude that Jesus had. Recall an instance from his life and ask yourself:

- how easy was it for him?
- what were the obstacles?
- what was necessary for overcoming them?

Recall an instance of your own experience of a holiday or some other time off when you got very close to another in that way:

- what helped bring that about?
- what qualities did both of you have to use?
- how important is the outcome?

What do such reflections suggest to you about the attractiveness and fruitfulness of our life in Christ, and of the God who is revealed in that?

Response

"Sabbath was a time for people to let God be God to them, to let God father them and mother them."

"All is ours" (1 Cor. 3:2).

*Lord, you don't want us to let routine or shallowness
    swallow us, because you want creation to be ours.
You want us to explore and reflect,
    to relax and to enjoy our physical and other powers,
    so that we can feel the wonder of your gift of creation,
    especially the gift of human kinship
    with our fellow women and men.*

*Help me to feel, on such occasions,
    my fellowship with you,
    loving promoter of all that is most human.*

Disagreements and Anger

⊱ Are Disagreements OK? ⊰

Experience

"We pretend that good families don't fight. They do. Everybody does. It is essential to fight for good health in the family. It gets things out into the open. But we need to learn to put ourselves back together—and many families never learn." (A therapist)

Do you find that "fighting" can be "essential for good health" in your family?

What are the best ways, in your family, of "putting ourselves back together"?

Reflection

"We know how to break up, but who the hell ever teaches us to make up?"

Many families do learn to make up. They may have a family policy that nobody goes to bed angry at another, or a mutual understanding that potentially explosive subjects get aired only at more favorable times: not just before going out or going to bed.

They may also develop ways of tacitly saying "That storm is now over."

How important is an atmosphere of peace for our development as Christians?

What best helps you to achieve that?

Response

"The glory of God is a man or woman fully alive" (Irenaeus, 2nd century).

Lord, you made me to be fully alive,
to get involved,
to try to sort things out,
to care,
to explore new avenues,
even though you knew I'd get some things wrong.

Help me to live up to this opportunity you have given me
and to respect it in others.

Teach me to be part of an orchestra,
not a one-person band,
even though false notes and clashes will occur.

❧ Two Cheers for My Anger ❧

Experience

I got furious at a friend for not returning my car when she promised—but later heard that the delay wasn't her fault. I "shoot from the hip." Why do I do that?

Partly a short fuse. "Inherited," I like to say.

That may make me shoot *too fast*. But why do I feel the urge to shoot *at all*?

Sometimes it's behavior I strongly disapprove of. I can't blame myself for that.

But other elements are less good. Sometimes it's not genuine indignation but my fear that my self-importance is being threatened. Sometimes I've not tried to understand—still less to forgive—the person who's angered me.

What feelings of anger in yourself do you consider to be right, and which do you regret?

For many of us it can be difficult to control our expression of anger. What works best for you?

In what cases or circumstances do you find that control to be particularly important?

Reflection

The irritable person who interprets harmless remarks as an insult obviously has a problem and makes relationships more difficult. So has the person who never feels anger, even at major injustices. Really living means involvement: not just with our minds and actions, but also with our *feelings*.

Jesus taught that the feeling of loving compassion was the central characteristic of God, of his own ministry, and of any true disciple (Matt. 18:23-34). He and his Father aren't passionless spectators. The very word for compassion meant "gut": they are involved at the "gut" level.

"God's like that," he said in his parables. "So am I. If you want to be really alive, you must be compassionate."

People's essential lovableness and their need should be felt deeply. So also should the selfish sabotage of opportunities for people's welfare and development. God is our "Father": a father who cares. Our lives are an invitation to be kin with God.

Drug barons clearly conduct such sabotage. But most cases are more subtle and "respectable." What should be the particular objects of your anger in your circumstances?

What could make that anger effective?

Response

Lord, you gave me fire.

> *You didn't make me to be tame and passionless,*
>> *like a faceless bureaucrat in some huge governmental agency.*

> *Help me to care.*

> *Help me open my mind and heart to the injustices that lurk beneath the surface of my world,*
>> *help me to share in your anger.*

> *Let me be fiery, Lord, but not harsh.*

> *Let me use my fire to do your work,*
>> *not be mastered by it and so disrupt your work.*

> *I love you, Lord, for your compassion, and also for your fire.*

Sexuality

❧ Thank God for My Sexuality ❧

Experience

The New Testament stresses that God loves us and saves us as bodily people (e.g., 1 Cor. 6:13-20).

My sexual activity can be no more than my self-gratification where my own pleasure is my only concern, and I want to draw the whole of what I see into myself.

Or it can be a way in which I break out of my aloneness and my depreciation of my body, to form an intimate faithful relationship, where our bodies play a central role in this bonding.

Then our sexual activity can be a way in which:

• we thank each other not only for the sexual act but also for each other's presence in the whole of our relationship.

• we reassure each other that each is wanted and appreciated and that we would like to stay together in the future.

• we partially or completely make up quarrels.

• we reinforce each other's masculine or feminine sexual identity.

What benefits have you experienced from your sexual activity?

Reflection

Not long ago Christianity's official approach to sexual activity was mainly a "policeman's" one: to guard against adultery and fornication.

But now that the insights of Scripture are being recovered, the focus has profoundly changed. Instead of a chiefly negative aim of avoiding sin, we are moving to an appreciation of the gift of our sexuality as:

• where men and women can become more fully the individuals we are, and yet profoundly share in achieving this and enjoying it (Genesis 2:18-24). Our divisiveness and lonesomeness are radically overcome.

• where our bodiliness comes to full fruition. Paul particularly insisted that our bodiliness is central to God's plans for us (1 Cor. 6:13-20).

Response

Our sexual activity, in all its aspects, is where we can especially find God.

Accept the invitation of Scripture to find God:

• in the beauty of the other, in the tenderness and stimulation of sexual foreplay, as our way of expressing our appreciation and delight in each other.

• in the emotional unity that the act of intercourse can express and foster.

> Lord, we often look for you in distant abstractions,
> but find you in sexual activity!
> We look for you as individual "souls,"
> but find you in the interplay of our bodies!

> As we turn to your Son we see more clearly
> that you are the healing, transforming power
> at the heart of our bodily lives,
> in our joy at sharing with each other,
> in our reconciling,
> in all our gratitude and tender care.

❧ Riding the Troughs ❧

Experience

I may find God in my sexual relationships when they are going well. But what about when they go badly?

We cannot remain at a peak-time indefinitely: the forces against that are too strong. Human sexuality is about the mutual affirmation of two *different* people.

The first months are easy. Each of us rides on the crest of the wave of the discovery that *I* am immensely attractive to the other.

Then comes the time when the gloss has worn off and our weaknesses and differences begin to grate. Sex can often become a routine, instead of an expression of our wanting to give love and pleasure.

We may pull back to a certain aloofness. The self-exposure necessary for real intimacy is too much of a threat, and emotionally it's too demanding.

To what extent has your relationship gone through such stages? What helped or hindered you then?

Reflection

Every form of life has its "downs."

Jesus' public life seems to have begun with a "high." He was a "sensation" in Galilee. He drew large crowds, and was invited to speak in the synagogue.

The rapid fall in his drawing-power did not come from a change in himself but from the superficiality of most people's interest and the thinness of their commitment to him.

He remained determined, in spite of everything, to continue to share completely and to remain vulnerable. He is "the full expression of the Father's being" (Hebrews 1:3).

As with Jesus, do our "downs" force us back to the bedrock of our relationship:

• the reality of our desire to share deep human feelings of love, fear, hope, joy and disappointment?

• our willingness to risk exposing our true selves to the other: really being the other's?

Response

> Lord, living with my guard down
>> isn't how I saw marriage at first.

> We foresaw no threat or disruption,
>> at least until the baby came.

> Now marriage sometimes looks like a trap
>> you've lured us into, Lord:
>> our weaknesses exposed to each other,
>> our differences grating, with plenty of rows.

> Or is it a clever ruse to lead us into a fuller life than we might
> have reached by ourselves:
>> learning to share the hopes and fears
>> across the differences,
>> learning to love and cherish the other:
>> someone different from myself,
>> drawing me out of myself, helping me rise from my
>> self-centeredness?

> Lord, you showed us yourself in Jesus:
>> help us to be like him and walk with him.

My Close Relationships

❧ True Love ❧

Experience

For most people, the greatest pleasures of all are being loved, and loving deeply another person.

When that happens, we feel good in ourselves because we gain a greater confidence, and we view more boldly and creatively our own personality and the challenges that face us.

A still richer part of this experience is our entering intimately into the life of another person. From the closed-in world of my own personality, I am opening myself to a whole new world of endless variety, depth, and possibilities of fulfillment, for in reaching out to another, I am reaching out potentially to all others. Within the whole of my adult life, that is the barrier I most need to cross.

What has *being loved* meant to you? Regarding your experience of *loving others*, we know that much of what is called "love" is not really that. Morton Kelsey has proposed three yardsticks to measure true love:

- not satisfied with being just an emotion
- continuing to love other human beings until they feel loved
- a mixture of concern, caring and action.

In the light of your own experience of true love, how important do you find these yardsticks? What others would you add?

Reflection

The most amazing thing about Christianity, and about God, is that true love is their *only* concern.

"Love, and do what you like," said St. Augustine. "The whole Law is summed up in one commandment: 'Love your neighbor'," said St. Paul (Galatians 5:14).

Christianity is about my finding my full self by entering into the deepest life of others.

Jesus' stories were largely to help people recognize God in his kindness and transforming power both in his own life and in their own lives, and to see this as the center of the human story. He presented that as a deeply human option, but not as an easy option.

We know that it takes time, sensitivity, patience and self-sacrifice "to love other human beings until they feel loved," and that being human includes standing up to the setbacks and the disappointments. Reflect on your own experience of this.

Response

What will chiefly inspire us to follow the path of love is:

    a. our experience of being loved and loving others
    b. our awareness of Jesus as our guide, friend and model.

In your own way, thank God for both of these. As you thank God for showing himself to us in Jesus, you could take Paul's "pen-portrait" of Jesus, as C.H. Dodd called it:

"This is what love is like. Love is never in a hurry, and is always kindness itself. It doesn't envy anybody at all, it never boasts about itself. It's never snobbish or rude or selfish. It's tough—it can face anything. And it never loses trust in God, or in men and women; it never loses hope; and it never gives in. Love holds good—everywhere, for everybody, forever (1 Cor. 13:4-8: Allan Dale's version OUP).

❧ Someone You Love Deeply ❧

Experience

Usually it goes easily at first between us. There is the delight at being loved; knowing we are special to each other.

But the intimacy makes us feel exposed to each other, weaknesses and all. Our differences become much more obvious; and we have to make a strong effort to handle them with humor and understanding more than with brittleness.

Then we know why St. Paul called it "the hard labor of love."

What are the big differences in your friendship that you had to handle and come to terms with positively?

Reflection

Our faith tells us that it is in both the *joy* and the *labor* of love that we find God: in our delighting in it *and* in our working at it. So we find God in the three elements of love:

in our giving and receiving AFFIRMATION
in our giving and receiving HEALING
in our taking pleasure in each other's GROWTH

Reflect on experiences you have had of giving or receiving one of those. Perhaps you were helped when you really needed that or were given a sign of support or affection, like a hug or a hand clasp, or some affectionate words?

Look at one of your close relationships as realistically as you can, including your differences. You may have found yourselves different in some of your feelings, needs or tastes, in your sense of humor or your body clock.

What is helping you handle your differences?

Are there other possible sources of help?

*Would your relationship be so deeply satisfying if it was always easy:
if we could find God in our lives as easily as we can lift food off the shelf
in the supermarket?*

Response

THE GIFT

Open your mind and heart more fully to the gift of this person,
and to your relationship with him/her being a chief way in which
God shows himself most personally to you.

> *You have done many things for us, O Lord our God,
>   there is no one like you!
> You have made many wonderful plans for us.
> I could never speak of them all—
>   their number is so great (Psalm 40:5).*

and THE DIFFICULTIES

A prayer from a man who had recently been at rock-bottom:

> *Let us give thanks to the Lord and Father of our Lord
>   Jesus Christ,
>   the merciful Father,
>   the God from whom all help comes!*

> *He helps us in all our troubles,
>   so that we can help others who have all kinds of troubles,
>   using the same help we ourselves have received from God.
>   (2 Cor. 1:3-4)*

Dependents

❧ Children ❧

Experience

In the 1920s, a boy suffered a brain injury at birth. It made it difficult for him to speak with clarity and he couldn't fully control his hands. This made him feel third-rate. He felt destined for failure.

He did badly at school until a teacher gave him the affirmation he needed. The boy's name was Morton Kelsey, now a highly-successful author. His comment on his experience is that "few of us grow to our potential unless we are loved."

Many parents are generous with material things. They want their children's "success." But Kelsey doubts whether much love usually goes with this. "I have talked with thousands of people. But only a few, no more than 10%, felt that their childhood homes were places where the springs of love flowed freely."

How far do you agree with Kelsey about the importance of love in a child's development?

What have you already done to make "the springs of love" flow freely, for children, or for others dependent on you? What have the results shown to you?

Reflection

1. Reflect on families you know that do take Jesus' commandment of love seriously.

Many who seem not to may be the victims of blindness. For example, men spend twice as much time with children as they did 20 years ago, but that's very often less than an hour a week.

2. Having people depend on us is a responsibility and can be a heavy one.

Jesus pictured Christian life as a farmer's work for a harvest, and in his time that work was tough.

3. "A parent's task during the teenage years is to change from a manager to a coworker and a friend." (U.S. Department of Health, Education and Welfare). Paul, the great apostle, treated his congregations above all as brothers and sisters.

4. A "commandment" can sound like mainly a restriction. But Jesus' one Law asks us to exploit the goldmine on which we all stand (Matt. 13:44-45).

Response

> How great are God's riches!
> How deep are his wisdom and knowledge!
>
> Who can understand his ways? As the scripture says,
> Who knows the mind of the Lord?
> Who is able to give him advice?
> Who has ever given him anything,
> so that he had to pay it back?
>
> For all things were created by him,
> and all things exist through him and for him.
>
> To God be the glory for ever! Amen (Romans 11:33-36).

❧ The Elderly ❧

Experience

You've only to think of 10 elderly people you know to realize how many ways there are of being old.

My friend Alan went off to Africa, at 76, to explore African civilization. My aunt, at 85, still goes on tough pilgrimages. For people like these, the Third Age is what the French like to call it: "the Age of Living."

In one typical city, 44% of the 60-80 age bracket were found to be potential volunteers or employees. All they needed was a bit of help with transport, expenses, and some flexibility in work schedules.

"Work," as Noel Coward said, "is much more fun than fun." Increasingly, this kind of fun can be enjoyed by many of the elderly, if we insist on some minor changes.

We're fast moving towards a time (2040) when one person in five will be a pensioner. Will we ensure that this time of life can be for half of them an "age of living"?

We all know old people who are not as fortunate as Alan and my aunt. There can be the increasingly hopeless struggle to continue living at home; the loneliness of being cut off, by lack of transport, from family and friends; or the sadness that naturally comes with decreasing powers and freedom of movement.

What are your own experiences of the elderly or of old age? Since these take many forms, you may like to take one aspect at a time. For instance:

• the person who has lost most of his/her powers. Life seems not to be worth living. Why must human life end in this way?

• the marvellous things many old people can do, and the wisdom and serenity they can contribute;

• the love, tenderness and unselfishness that looking after or helping the elderly can bring out in us;

• our responsibilities in these matters.

Reflection

Old age is always a bad time to some extent, and can be severely so. We'll reflect on such experiences later (pages 33 and 34).

Our response to the elderly can help to free us from our selfishness and help us to be more on God's wavelength, as Jesus revealed through his own life and his parables:

• the practical help, even against great obstacles
• the tenderness, compassion, and desire to help and heal.

In your experience, can old age develop in old and young a sense of mutual interdependence and of our dependence on God's love and care?

Response

In a prison in Ephesus, hourly expecting a death sentence, St. Paul could celebrate with his friends the God at the heart of all things. Let us make his prayer ours:

May you always be joyful in your union with the Lord. I say it again: rejoice! Show a gentle attitude towards everyone. The Lord is coming soon. Don't worry about anything, but in all your prayers ask God for what you need, always asking him with a thankful heart. And God's peace, which is far beyond human understanding, will stand guard over your hearts and minds.
(Philippians 4:4-7)

Good Friends

⚜ Good Friends: How Important? ⚜

Experience

Few things are more likely to rouse our sympathy than to hear that a person is "friendless."

That's not because we're starry-eyed about friendship. We know that "friends" can let us down and that much so-called friendship is only skin-deep.

Why, then, does friendlessness sound like a death sentence?

"It's not good for the man to live alone" (Genesis 2:18). Each of us is *an individual*. We have the right, and the task, of becoming our true and unique self. But we've found so often that we achieve that largely *through friendship*.

That's confirmed by our experience of our sexuality, of family life, and other kinds of interdependence. And for many of us the crown of that experience is what good friends have meant for our happiness and development.

How important to you are good friends?

What makes them important to you, both for what you give as well as receive?

Reflection

We often hear that our century trivializes friendship. That's often true.

But it also opens up to us a wider range of real friendship: beyond the limits of locality, race, class and nationality.

Since we may feel close to our friend as him or herself—not just as "one of us"—we may have a truer experience of friendship, and find that experience very good.

Scripture shows how central is that experience to our discovery of God. The purpose of our lives is to be human projections of God; but the Genesis story makes clear that we can only do that as male and female, not as lone individuals.

The whole of the New Testament makes so clear that God is found only in close "friendship" or "fraternity"—the words, significantly, are interchanged!

The *kind of friendship* is made clear:

> *It's not exclusive or self-seeking (Luke 14:12).*
> *It is warm, generous, and joyfully celebrated (Luke 15:11f).*
> *But it's not soft or superficial: a friend stays loyal,*
>   *whatever the cost (Luke 12:4; 11:5-8)*
> *The test of a friend isn't nice words or feelings,*
>   *but a love that wants to build the other up (1 Cor. 8:1).*

In such friendship we see reflected, and are transformed by, the Friend and Father of all.

Response

> *God be in my head, and in my understanding;*
> *God be in my eyes, and in my looking;*
> *God be in my mouth, and in my speaking;*
> *God be in my heart, and in my thinking;*
> *God be at my end, and at my departing. (Old Sarum Primer)*

❧ Born for Friendship? ❧

Experience

"One of the major cultural events of our era is the determination by many men and women to build a new world in which friendship replaces fear and force as the fabric of human society."

At your work, in your neighborhood, in what you hear and see in the media, etc., do you find that view of a sociologist to be true for many people?

How important is friendship for you?

Reflection

We don't count a friendship a real one unless both people share quite a lot of themselves. They're not only willing to give help when needed; they also share their thoughts and feelings.

Some people seem unwilling to take the risk. They lead private, lonely lives.

Most of us *do* take that risk. There will probably be times of turbulence, pain, anxiety; but we reckon it's worth it.

We discover *ourselves*. We find that to another person we are lovable, warts and all. We also find we were made for fellowship, because we discover that appreciating and exploring human life is richer if we share them with another.

Above all, we discover *the other*. By discovering that *someone else* is lovable we raise the stakes on a wider field, for if one besides myself is found to be lovable, then could many others be, if only I really knew them?

We enter into a different way of experiencing things, a different way of responding to them. Our friend's stance to life isn't the same as ours, and yet we respect and love it. The rich diversity of human life is becoming clearer.

But it's not just *knowing about* the other that friendship consists of. There's no friendship without commitment. You give yourself to the other.

God's "Kingdom" is about our entering into life in the most realistic way possible. Friendship is its way; commitment is its thrust; costly mutual service its approach; a loyalty meal its chief expression; shared joy its aim. And it embraces all the human family, for all barriers are down (Gal. 3:28).

Response

Lord, where would I be without my friendships?
It's true that some of them are a bit phoney.
The warm greetings are a custom we've fallen into,
*   we don't really know one another.*

But with the real friendships it's not like that,
I've shared people's experiences, sometimes of
*   doubt and difficulty,*
*   and seen their courage and goodness in that*
*   and realized this is my friend!*

I look around at the world you have given us and hear your
Word to us: "You are born for friendship."

Loving Father, I thank you.
Help me use your gift for the joy of all.

The Weekend

❧ The Opportunities ❧

Experience

Imagine life *without* weekends.

There would be nothing to break up time into weeks. Less chance to relax with those close to us and get away from the treadmill. Little time to take stock of where we are or to consider the future.

What do you most appreciate about your weekends?
What are the chief opportunities they give you?

Reflection

For many of us, the most obvious opportunity in our weekend is to sleep in and relax. The pace of modern life makes that important.

As we think of the other opportunities, we realize that we have *more freedom of choice* than when we're at work. Of course that freedom is limited: there's the shopping and the chores. But it's largely *our* values which decide which opportunities we'll take up and which we'll let go. In our decisions, much of our personal stance to life is being expressed and even formed.

So we can reflect on the opportunities our weekend gives us from two points of view:

1) Which of the opportunities are we taking, like relaxation, time for family and friends, sharing the chores, time to reflect?

2) Are there some opportunities of the weekend that I should take up more wholeheartedly?

Is there someone close to me I should take more time with? Should I relax more?

Are there important areas of my life which are "on automatic" or are superficial, so that reflection is vital to make them as human and fruitful as I would like them to be?

Response

You could pray for those with whom you spend your weekends:

> *I ask God from the wealth of his glory*
> *   to give you power*
> *   through his Spirit*
> *   to be strong in your inner selves.*
>
> *I pray that Christ will make his home in your hearts*
> *   through faith.*
>
> *I pray that you may have your roots and foundation in love,*
> *   so that you,*
> *   together with all God's people,*
> *   may have the power to understand how broad and long,*
> *   how high and deep,*
> *   is Christ's love.*
>
> *May we always be humble, gentle and patient,*
> *   showing our love by being tolerant with one another,*
> *   doing our best to preserve the unity which the Spirit gives*
> *   by means of the peace that binds us together.*
>
> *I ask this of the Lord of all,*
> *   who works through all,*
> *   and is in all (Ephesians 3:16-4:6).*

❧ Sunday ❧

Experience

Not long ago Sunday was widely experienced as a rather joy-less experience. Sports were forbidden. So were the livelier hob-bies and entertainments. Sunday worship threw little light, for many Christians, on God's loving presence in our lives.

With the help of Scripture we are re-discovering the true pur-pose of Sunday.

Sunday was the day when the local Christian community as-sembled to say "Yes" to the power of the risen Jesus in their lives. They had experienced God's regenerating power through their partnership with Jesus. They wanted to say "Yes" to that: a "Yes" of gratitude and commitment.

They experienced that power in each other's gifts. As the local Christian community they treasured and used that power in part-nership. Sunday was for celebrating all this together and for working out how best to use those gifts in the future.

Sunday, therefore, wasn't for *reducing* life but for *realizing its full potential*. Together we look at what we've got, so that we can use it better in the weekdays. Both as individuals and as congre-gations we are moving towards this richer use of Sundays.

What greater opportunities have you seen in the last 10 years? What are your hopes for the next 10 years?

Here is a checklist, to which you can add:

• Christians gathering for a common purpose ("church" = as-sembly)

• Worship: our celebrating the power of the risen Jesus in us now (on Sunday we look at our past and present)

• Worship: our committing ourselves to further involvement in this story. Sunday is the "first day of the week," when we joyfully face our task of helping to humanize the life around us, in our everyday activities.

• as an assembly, we get to know each other better, and work out the practical details of what we can do.

Reflection

Sunday has little chance of being these things for us:

• if we merely swim with the tide

• if we aren't aware of our Christian dignity as partners with Jesus in God's work for the world

• if we don't realize that the Jesus movement is about overcoming "dead" things with God's fullness of life.

Reflect on people you know who have helped you to overcome one or more of these things.

In what ways would you like to develop your use of Sunday this year?

Response

Lord, you help us to rediscover the excitement of Sunday.

We made it so dull. We just didn't understand what your Word was saying to us.

Now we're beginning to pray like a sports team, certain of victory, as we meet before a match.

You're there in the "match." That's what we celebrate with you, Lord, on Sunday. In my work, my family life, and my work for other people, you are bringing life out of death.

Through us you are leading all humankind toward God's glorious future.

My Neighbors

❧ Who Needs Neighbors? ❧

Experience

"They borrow things and don't return them."

"Their children are a menace."

"With their different social habits they don't fit in."

"Their noisy parties."

Plenty of people feel they *don't* need their neighbors: at any rate, not the ones they've got.

Why do others really value their neighbors? For Joe and Jean it's because their whole little town is neighborly: it's almost second-nature in Dalry (which I visit every year) to be helpful to each other.

For Mike and Tricia, it's because they and their children take active parts in local sports. For others, it's shared involvement in a school, a church, an activity, or a street.

What has it been like for you to try to love your neighbor? Have you discovered some good things and some bad things in your trying to relate to them as a Christian?

Reflection

Obviously, we can't value our neighbors unless we're open to giving them our respect.

By what yardsticks do I decide whether or not I will be open to the goodness in this man, woman or child, who may disturb me by differences or demands?

The yardsticks of Scripture:

THE STORY OF THE GOOD SAMARITAN (Luke 10:30-37)

- a story about being a neighbor

- turns on "being moved with compassion" (a word virtually reserved for God in Jesus' time) and on giving practical help to someone who, by all current Jewish yardsticks, should have been treated with contempt.
- ends: "Go, and do the same yourself." That's what the Kingdom of God is all about.

JESUS' AIMS

- to call the whole People of God to become one again
- so that the whole human race could overcome its disunity and its "darkness"

Response

Lord, you befriended beggars and even outcasts.
You passionately desired their healing.

You wanted to show God's work for human wholeness.
You want my life to be a light like yours;
you want me to share in that wholeness.

Help me to treasure and set my life by the good news
that inspired you.
Open my eyes to the humanity all around me,
which speaks of you.

❧ Gateways to Good News ❧

Experience

You are trying to treat as your neighbor even people who might disturb you or make demands on you. Scripture has convinced you that such a way of life is God's "Good News," where he shows us our humanity more richly.

One thing such an attitude does is to make us more open to people we have kept away from simply because we didn't know them or because we were unnecessarily suspicious of them. We become more open, more trusting people, and more compassionate about human weakness. We *will* be let down, but we try to see this in the context of something wider and more important.

Consider your experience of trying to love your neighbor: both the good things you've discovered and your being let down. What have you learned from these experiences?

Reflection

What has helped you towards this openness to others?

THE FAMILY

"Families either teach respect or they don't. In our practice we rarely find a family where one member respects people and the others don't." (A family counselor)

When you were a child, did your family teach respect? What have been other important influences on your attitudes to neighbors?

THE NEIGHBORHOOD

In Dalry, where Joe and Jean live, it's second nature to get to know your neighbors and to help them. But it can be very different in places where people have little in common, and where there's no neighborhood activity to break down barriers. Even your next-door neighbors, for years, seem like distant icebergs.

What in the character of your neighborhood, or through some initiative or accident, has helped you appreciate some of the neighbors more? What conclusions do you draw from that?

Response

1. Thank God for specific neighbors:

> • who have helped you, and perhaps stood by you in difficult times

> • whom you discovered, perhaps to your surprise, are people you like

> • who widen the horizons of yourself and/or your family

> • whom you have helped

> • who have shown you something about handling life which you value: like enduring great misfortune or coping with anger or opposition.

2. Thank God for all that has helped you become more open to your neighbors.

3. In the light of Jesus' *Good Samaritan* story, write down a way in which you will help your family or your neighborhood be more responsive to the neighbors:

_____

_____

_____

_____

Our Neighborhood

⁓ What's Your Neighborhood to You? ⁓

Experience

If you were to ask 20 people from different areas what their neighborhoods meant to them, you'd be likely to get quite a range of answers.

On the one side there could be some who have no sense of belonging and who have little interest in getting to know their neighbors. On the other, there could be those who tell you of street parties or of dances to raise money for neighborhood purposes. They may talk of warm relationships that resulted and some neighborhood projects.

You would notice that the answers could depend partly on whether the interviewee is married or single. The latter may have more need of a friendly neighborhood and more time to contribute to it.

People's goodwill may be evident. They would *like* to help make their neighborhood, more friendly, more fun, and more supportive. But with their long hours of work, and the claims of family and other interests, they may feel they have no spare energy. Or the electronic world of TV and the home computer can seem more inviting.

> *What kind of neighborhood do you live in?*
> *Is there much sense of identity?*
> *Is there much contact between people?*

Reflection

If we had access to *all* the data about our neighborhood, we'd probably find it a sleeping giant.

51

Of course there'd be many people with unmet needs of friendship and of a sense of belonging. There would also be the missed opportunities for fun, and for developments that could enrich many lives.

Have we, as Christians, an important role here?

One obstacle to our neighborhood's development may be people's *mobility*; but our local church has *some stability*.

Another obstacle may be the lack of *an initial spark* to get bold action; our church has *some enterprising people*.

Another obstacle may be a weak sense of local identity; could we *join another organization* in helping to nurture that—or is our own church's identity the only one we care about?

Christ wants his local church to be his "embodiment," so that he becomes really accessible to those around. The chief way is our loving our neighbor. How far can that be successful without our also loving and humbly serving the neighborhood?

Response

> Lord, you want me to pray because
> you want me to take the time
> to dream with you.
>
> This week I'll dream with you about some of my neighbors:
> elderly people without a car,
> young mothers tied to the household and child care,
> youths thrown out of their homes,
> people no one befriends.
>
> Thy Kingdom come.
>
> Lord, in my small way, I'll join you in bringing your dream
> to life.

❧ Neighborliness in Practice ❧

Experience

When you bring into your prayers people in need, you want to help them. Sometimes as an individual you can do that. But quite often you lack the time or resources.

The only chance of adequate help may be from the "giant" rising more fully from its sleep.

To see what that would be like, we have to "dream." How many great enterprises could have begun without people dreaming, whether of liberty, power, or some other compelling goal?

Recall some of the dynamics of neighborhood life, which may need to become stronger?

SELF-HELP ACTIVITIES. The initial thrust usually comes from our own activities, like our inviting the people around us to bring their brooms for a morning clean-up, or to some social activity we are arranging. Through such activities our relationships grow. These lead to further activities. Some of these can become sturdy annual events.

COMMUNITY DEVELOPMENT. Those fairly piecemeal activities can lead to something more deliberate. The members of the neighborhood are enabled to consider the local needs and how they might be met. Now *everyone* is encouraged to "dream": to listen to each other and to become more aware of people's needs.

Then they join to see what their own efforts, and various bodies, could do to help.

VOLUNTARY ASSOCIATIONS. We're increasingly sensing ourselves as a body with shared goals.

One route to fulfill one of these is to set up a voluntary association for that purpose. It might be for combating delinquency or the use of drugs, or to set up some amenity. It will co-opt professional help but also needs to stay close to the feelings and views of the people it represents.

53

How much of this kind of interlocking structure is already in place in your neighborhood?

To what extent is it helpful—or, to what extent could it be helpful?

Reflection

Jesus' story shows the Samaritan (*not* "one of us"!) as having God-like attitudes but also as very practical. The wounded man needed rest, medicine, food, transport and money. Without them, "compassion" would have been empty.

In the light of the realities of your neighborhood, what practical conclusions do you draw from Jesus' story for:

 a. your local church?
 b. yourself?

Response

You could write here:

 a. some developments you would like to see in your
  neighborhood over the next three years:

  _____
  _____

 b. what you will do towards that:

  _____
  _____

 c. whom you hope will benefit:

  _____
  _____

My Decisions

❧ How Important? ❧

Experience

Our decisions can be important:

because they have important consequences: the atmosphere I try to form in my family, for example, will have a life-long effect; so will my choice of spouse. Decisions about my job, my choice of friends and my health are also important.

because they may be reached in a significant way: after a lot of thought and prayer, perhaps; or as a decision shared with my spouse, or even with the whole family.

because they may be an important expression of myself: what makes me the person I am are my values and my aims. Some of my decisions express those deeply.

Reflection

Most of us have a strong sense that *I* steer this ship. To a large extent, my decisions are important.

Our Christian faith confirms this and extends it immensely.

I am *a partner of God*, through Jesus, in his work of transformation. The "harvest" I'm helping to work for will be very great and very joyful.

I am that partner as *the free responsible person I am*, using my particular "gift," conscious of God's presence, and seeking myself to be transformed into a more human person.

I am a member of *Christ's body*, called to help our human world rediscover its kinship, so that sharing my decisions, where possible, takes on still more value.

Yet I steer this ship to a limited extent. Events I can't control will send it off the course I planned. Eventually my ship will break on the rocks of death.

But my faith tells me that these are only apparent limitations. The particular decisions I make are important, but only in the context of "Thy will be done."

My wisdom and my kindness are limited. But, with God as my loving partner, the effect of what I do is not.

Response

"When the right time finally came, God sent his Son, so that we might become God's sons and daughters. To show that you are that, God sent the Spirit of his Son into our hearts, the Spirit who cries out, 'Father, my Father'." Since you are his son or daughter, God will give you all that he has for his children. Now you know God—or should I say, now God knows you" (Galatians 4:4-9).

> Lord, you show me, through the resurrection power of your Son,
>   that I am loved.
> I'm heir and partner;
> I am made for fruitfulness.
> That's what you wanted for me:
>   so much that your Son died for that.
>
> "I know you. You know me.
> We're in this together—for harvest."
>
> Help me to understand better what harvest we're aiming for,
> Help me share more deeply your love and faithfulness for all,
>   so that my decisions will bear much fruit.

56

❧ Finding the Way ❧

Experience

What decisions have you made today?

Many may be hard to remember: just habits or reactions, like the choice of a drink or a route.

Even with the real decisions, you may regard few as important. It's not every day we buy a home, choose a career, or start a deep friendship!

What changes the list from fairly commonplace to interesting are our "invisible" decisions. What gives my life force and shape aren't my off-the-cuff choices but my ongoing commitments. "I'll make a go of my marriage." "I want a good life for my kids." "I really want to be successful in my career, or in this interest."

It's my "invisible" decisions that make me the person I am.

What personal loyalties, what aims or values, are shaping the main contours of your life? What decisions have they particularly influenced?

Reflection

Through my commitments my life gets its shape, its thrust, its sense of purpose.

They also connect me up with something wider than my individual self. I know that commitments, in the long haul, are not easy. In spite of that I decide to stand for things beyond my own pleasure, like faithfulness, love, integrity and justice.

Is this the most remarkable thing about most of us? We not only go beyond the boundaries of our individual selves, but we also try to direct our lives by what we discover when we do that. We find a goodness that transcends us in a person, a principle, or a cause. Only by committing myself to such as these do I find real value in my life.

What is the basic Christian commitment? The center of the Christian Good News—and so of all Christian morality—is Jesus' experience of God, which made him want to create a context in which all men and women could also find such a God in *their* lives. He wants us to be able to face ourselves, our weaknesses, our whole experience of life, with confidence, so that we are free to turn to others with openness and love. "To make that experience of life more widely available is the main task of Christendom." (Paul Hoffmann)

How important to you—and others—are your basic commitments behind your decisions?

How do you form and deepen them?

What persons, principles and causes particularly illumine for you the meaning and value of your life?

Response

> *Teach me your ways, O Lord;*
>   *make them known to me.*
> *Teach me to live according to your truth,*
>   *for you are my God, who saves me.*
>
> *I always trust in you.*
>
> *Remember, O Lord, your kindness and constant love*
>   *which you have shown long ago.*
> *In your constant love and goodness,*
>   *remember me, Lord! (Psalm 25:4-7)*

Money

❧ The Plus Side ❧

Experience

The lines and empty shelves in the shops of Eastern Europe remind us of what our relative affluence gives us in our country.

We have food in our freezer, and warmth and comfort in our homes. We have TV, a video, a music center, and holidays away.

Our ancestors would have regarded this as luxury. But money has brought us even more than that. It gives us medical care, longer life, education, and a wider awareness of our world.

Of the things that our Western affluence has brought you, which do you value most?

Which has the deepest impact on the quality of your life?

Reflection

"God looked at everything he had made, and he was very pleased" (Genesis 1:31).

"God created human beings, making them to be like himself. He blessed them and said, 'Have children, so that your descendants will live all over the earth and exercise dominion over it'" (Genesis 1:27-28).

My relative affluence gives me opportunities to understand better what God has made, and to be "very pleased."

It also gives me opportunities to share responsibility and creativity in our "dominion" over the earth, sometimes at cost to myself—in Jesus' way.

Reflect on ways in which our Western standard of living has helped you better appreciate God's creation.

Response

1. *Lord, I thank you for showing me the wonder of my vocation as a human being.*

   *Help me to embrace it more creatively,
   more generously,
   so as to become the kind of person you are calling
   me to be.*

2. *O Lord, our Lord,
   your greatness is seen in all the world!
   When I look at the sky, which you have made,
   at the moon and the stars, which you set in their places—
   what is humankind, that you think of us;
   mere men and women, that you care for them?
   Yet you made them inferior only to yourself,
   you crowned them with glory and honor.
   You appointed them ruler over everything you made;
   you placed them over all creation (Psalm 8).*

3. List some of the ways in which you could use what you have been given to correspond better with our human vocation:

   money:

   _____

   _____

   talents:

   _____

   _____

   developing your own gifts:

   _____

   _____

❧ The Minus Side? ❧

Experience

"Problems of sexual relationships do not produce the greatest number of marriage conflicts and divorces. But problems of money do. Hostility generated because two people cannot come to an agreement as to a fair distribution of their income breaks up more homes than anything else. . . It's known as the number one stress in family life today."

Is this, to any degree, a problem for you?

Morton Kelsey (quoted above) believes that *this problem can be largely eliminated when people share feelings and relate equally.* How does your experience support that view?

Reflection

Money isn't just a cause of dispute in families. It can also wound deeply the capacity to accept others.

In addition, it is often a real worry. In spite of real income increases, over 40% of people worry frequently that their family income won't meet the expenses. They feel that to accept a lower lifestyle would mean personal failure. Their economic prospects in retirement is a related cause for anxiety.

What help can come from our main Christian perspectives for coping with these problems?

• Christianity is about *sharing*, or *community*. Families cope with these problems when they share openly their fears, decisions, values and budgeting: share not just the knowledge of the finances, but also the responsibility.

• Christianity is also about *finding your true self through playing your part in God's work for the world*: something wider and deeper than we can see. That doesn't abolish our fears, but can help us get them in proportion.

Response

Lord, your Son and his friends knew all about boats.
I know about money: the experience is much the same.

Sometimes it's like a big catch. I have a sense of my own power. I
enjoy people's admiration: the rest of the world are just onlookers.
Me and my satisfaction are centerstage.

Then there's the storm of difficulty or danger,
or the cold wind of anxiety.
Then we huddle together, find our kinship;
we're thrown back to trust in your loving care.

It's a tough way, dear Lord, of teaching me that there is no truly
human existence without community;
that the only road to true humanity lies
through sharing with each other.

Help us find our true selves, and you, through sharing and trust.

Help me to use money with your wisdom,
on both stormy and bright days.

Good Times

❧ Appreciation ❧

Experience

What the Hebrews discovered through their experiences was that, in a dangerous, hard world, their God saved them. There was evil and pain; there was failure and death. But, even in the midst of all that, a wise and loving God was in charge.

Through what people found in Jesus, they saw this still more strongly. The chief characteristic of God was "bringing even the dead to life," "bringing all things to good" (Romans 4:17; 8:28). Paul regularly takes whole sections of his life of arduous service and responds with a shout of triumphant wonder and thanks (what was called a "eucharist").

Are there some sections of your life where you may have experienced some pain, failure or struggle, as well as some good things, but where sooner or later you recognized the God of those characteristics? Did that help you appreciate more the good things you have experienced?

Reflection

In Scripture and in our tradition, prayer is where I say "yes" to the whole story in which God and I are involved. Prayer is like a couple taking an evening off to celebrate their life together. They revel in all that love and fruitfulness, through the bright days and the dark.

In prayer the good times have a relevance even beyond the immediate happiness they can give us. Things like a new baby; success in sports or work; a good holiday; a happy evening with friends: these are relevant because *God has made us for happiness. In them his character and our destiny are revealed.*

Prayer is where we not only rejoice in our good times but also rejoice in what they say about all our futures.

This view of prayer is only now becoming better known, as we get closer to Scripture. How far does it help you better appreciate your good times?

Response

We can say this as our response both to:

- what God has made us;
- the destiny he has given us.

I will proclaim your greatness, my God and king;
I will thank you for ever.

People will tell about all your goodness
and sing about your kindness.
The Lord is loving and merciful,
slow to become angry and full of constant love.

He is good to everyone
and has compassion on all he made.
The Lord is faithful to his promises,
and everything he does is good.
He helps those who are in trouble;
he lifts those who have fallen.

All living things look hopefully to you,
and you give them food when they need it.
You give them enough
and satisfy the needs of all (Psalm 145).

⚘ The Difference Looking Makes ⚘

Experience

You find that something has happened that you are sure will be excellent news for a friend. Delighted about your friend's good fortune, you tell him or her this news. "Oh, yes," your friend might say, unmoved and not very interested.

To most of my good times, my response has had quite a high proportion of that kind of attitude. I have a holiday, visit a friend, attend an interesting meeting; I have a walk in the country, listen to music, understand better or help some person.

Part of my response is appreciation: I do enjoy such things. But part of it is "Oh, yes," as I move on to other things.

What have been your best good times in the last 12 months?

How far has your response been "Oh, yes"?

Reflection

A couple are walking through a bit of the country, enjoying this "sweet special rural scene." A train sweeps by, and to its passengers—if they look at all—it's no more than a momentary backdrop.

We can't *see* if we don't look. We can't *feel* unless we give our emotions a chance to respond.

Are we really living if we don't look and respond?

Prayer is looking, and responding. Not looking *up there*, to a different world; but looking *here*, in this world. And our good times, if we do look, are radiant with God.

> *The world is charged with the grandeur of God.*
> *It will flame out, like shining from shook foil.*
> *The Holy Ghost over the bent*
> *World broods with warm breast and with ah! bright wings.*

Response

1. Could you make a habit of reflecting every week, or every evening, on your recent good times:

That visit to a friend; that game; that walk; that party; whatever:

- what goodness in it did you well recognize at the time?

- what goodness in it do you see well only in retrospect?

- are there ways in which you could appreciate it better in the future?

> *How good it is to give thanks to you, O Lord,*
> *to sing in your honor, O Most High God,*
> *to proclaim your constant love every morning*
> *and your faithfulness every night,*
> *with the music of stringed instruments*
> *and with melody on the harp.*
> *Your mighty deeds, O Lord, make me glad;*
> *because of what you have done, I sing for joy.*
> *(Psalm 92:1-4)*

Bad Times

❧ How Bad? ❧

Experience

"Bad times have been abolished in all civilized countries." At least that is today's fashionable belief.

Illness is taken care of by diet, jogging and medicine; guilt and frustration by psychiatrists. Death is an embarrassing exception, so it's alluded to only at funerals—and even there "discreetly."

True, a positive approach is to be welcomed, and also the use of modern skills. But "abolishing" bad times prevents us from coping with experiences that all of us have.

Reflect on bad times you coped with successfully. What helped you do that?

Reflection

Bad times are part of being human. What happens when we confront them?

WE SEEK A SENSE OF PROPORTION. Yes, I *do* have bad times. I have my regrets, my failures, my frustrations, and my pain. Sometimes they blot out all the rest.

But in other circumstances I can look at the other side of the balance-sheet as well: pleasure from love and friendship, family life, children, food and drink, and many other things.

When you do that, does your view, even in a bad time, alter?

WE FACE FAILURE OR LOSS. We know that such experiences can be devastating. A teenager put this in poignant form when his father suddenly lost his job: "It was like he wasn't a good person anymore."

The damage that results can be deep and long-lasting. But suppose I decide to fill in *both* sides of the balance sheet?

To live as a human being, I have to take my part in the human story as a person with limited powers, and with a limited time span before death. There are strong elements in all of us that tend to blind us to this indispensable awareness.

If everything went our way, and if death did not exist, would this lead to things like arrogance that would make us much less human?

WE FACE PAIN In front of the disaster of a huge earthquake, or of constant and intense pain in someone we know, words cannot cope.

But is that true of most pain? Many of the pains we get are nature's warning signals, say of overwork, overweight, or some other kind of stress: signals that we need.

If we think human life should consist of individuals doing their own thing, in an effortlessly successful way, with no deep relationship with others, then pain is all bad. But if it's about growth in human relationships, solidarity, and compassion, is there another side of this mystery? "Pain delivers us from narrow self-concern and makes us feel our oneness with other human beings."

Response

> *We can turn to Jesus and let his life in Palestine*
> *and his life in each of us*
> *now speak to us:*
> *about narrow self-concern*
> *about our oneness with other human beings.*

❧ Our Suffering and Jesus ❧

Experience

Jesus' experience. Quite early in his public life, Jesus saw the probability of his rejection. Everyone knew what the Romans did to "fake Messiahs."

Undeterred, he went right on: not fearfully, but with joy. The warm happy parties; the stories that radiated an appreciation of the world he knew: in the teeth of obvious failure, Jesus lived like one certain of triumph.

Part of Jesus' way of coping lay in his accepting positively the bodily realities of our existence, even though their meaning is partly beyond human understanding.

What made that trust possible was his awareness of God's power *in these realities.*

He called that power *GOD'S KINGDOM,* or *RULE.*

Paul's experience. Paul also lived like one certain of triumph, in spite of much suffering and failure. For him, Christian life was being joined with Jesus. Sharing in Jesus' destiny and work was the supremely desirable crown of human life.

That destiny and that work were "bodily." It wasn't saving *from* the body, but bringing to fulfillment *a bodily person.* Just as Jesus' life was "about" the physical and social realities of the Palestine of his day, so Paul's partnership with Jesus was "about" the realities of his day.

Like Jesus, Paul believed that God's creative power or "gracious kindness" is at the very heart of our experience, and is already breaking in, not in some detached faculty like a "soul," but in the humanity we feel and love: suffering, joy and all! Already we have the first taste and pledge of the full victory to come.

What experience have you had, in your own life or in others, of this power? Even in suffering?

Reflection

Paul is aware of:
> comfort in the midst of suffering (2 Cor. 1:5)
> life in the midst of death (2 Cor. 4:10)

Henceforth,
> suffering is a suffering with Christ (Romans 8:17)
> because all suffering is embraced by God's saving power and takes place in the light of the coming glory of God.

Response

Christ was raised to life.
Who, then, can separate us from the love of Christ?
Can trouble do it, or hardship or persecution,
> *or hunger or poverty,*
> > *or danger or death?*

No, in all these things we have complete victory through him who loved us.

For I am certain that nothing can separate us
> *from his love:*
> > *neither death nor life,*
> > *neither angels nor other heavenly rulers or powers,*
> > *neither the present nor the future,*
> > *neither the world above nor the world below—*
> *there is nothing in all creation that will ever be able to separate us from the love of God*
> *which is ours through Christ Jesus our Lord*
> > > > *(Romans 8:34-39).*

Our World—and our Grandchildren

ઝ "A New Groundswell" ઝ

Experience

For centuries the only thing that changed in the world for most people was the weather—and you couldn't control it. Today we still can't control the weather, but most other things we can.

It's like steering a big ship. You touch the tiller, but it takes time for the ship to swing onto a different course.

Factors affecting our journey include:

WATER. Over half the people in the Third World have no source of safe water to drink. This contributes to 80% of disease and kills perhaps 50,000 people a day.

FOOD. In 1930 our world contained 2000 million people; in 1975, 4000 million; in 2000 or so, about 6900 million. At this writing, some 440 million are "chronically undernourished," and already there is a death from inadequate diet every 8 seconds. In parts of many cities 1 in 4 children die of malnutrition before they are 5. We have no clear idea how we can feed the 8000 million people our children and grandchildren will have to cope with if present Third World population trends continue (multiplying twice as fast as in the affluent nations).

ENERGY. Our present affluence comes from our huge consumption of energy, which is mostly unrenewable. Even if we started working immediately on policies to cope with this, it would still be a race against time.

In spite of the size and urgency of the problem, we are not powerless. For example, none of these would be very difficult:

- providing piped water and some other essential services would cost about $50 million for 600,000 people.
- steps could be taken to enable the Third World to reduce its population increase by up to 50%.

71

- the rich nations could import more from Third World countries and pay higher prices for it, as well as sell our own manufactured goods at less than their full economic prices. This, and long-term interest loans, would be indispensable for breaking out of the poverty trap.

What kind of "ship" will our children and our grandchildren be steering?

Reflection

Who holds the key?

1. "If the planet's rush to self-destruction is to be slowed in time, Mr. Bush may be the last President to have that opportunity." (*New York Times*, Nov. 28, 1988)

2. "The new groundswell of environmental concern." (NYT)

"People will vote 80 to 20 for a tougher Clean Air Act, but 80 to 20 against if you ask them to devote 20 minutes a year to having their car emissions inspected." (NYT)

"It's going to have to bubble up; that is the way policy gets made. The last people to get the idea are the visibly responsible leaders, because they are too visible to take responsibility for change."

Response

Lord, when our grandchildren pray "Thy Kingdom come,"
may the world we leave them
be good ground
for your transforming power.

Who Will Save
❧ Our Grandchildren a World? ❧

Experience

We know what kind of world our grandchildren will be facing if there isn't strong action soon.

We can imagine how they would feel about us if they had to try to cope with a world where there is double the present population, much less energy, and less land on which to grow food. We can guess how much political stability there might be in such a world. And this isn't to mention problems from pollution and the ozone layer.

There *is* a groundswell of concern. The world is waking up to the problem, and in that lies our hope.

The Scripture insight is that human fulfillment comes only from an involvement in God's work for the world that is responsible and loving.

Is that view taken by most Christians you know? If not, why is that so?

What is your local church, or local community, contributing?

Reflection

1. How important is it that we Christians strongly back that Scripture insight?

What more should we do?

2. JESUS' ANNOUNCEMENT, IN THE NAZARETH SYNAGOGUE, ABOUT THE WORK OF GOD IN OUR WORLD:

The Spirit of the Lord is upon me,
because he has chosen me to bring good news to the poor.
He has sent me to proclaim liberty to the captives
and recovery of sight to the blind;
to set free the oppressed

and announce that the time has come
when the Lord will save his people.

Then he sat down and said to them: "This passage of Scripture has come true today" (Luke 4:16-21).

How can my life be part of this?

Response

Lord, you have made so many things!
How wisely you made them all!
The earth is filled with your creatures.
All of them depend on you
to give them food when they need it.
You provide food and they are satisfied (Psalm 104).

You share with us humans your lordship
through our union with Jesus,
a lordship that is respectful of all you made,
caring for each thing's welfare,
courageous and loving, like your Son.
What gift is there that is nobler and more God-like:
to be loving stewards of this good world?

Through the challenges of today, Lord, you are asking us
to come of age.
Help me, and all of us, to respond.

Your Job

❧ Your Job: Good or Bad? ❧

Experience

In the world of work, in the 1990's, something is stirring.

In the past there was a high wall round our work saying: "No God here." We could find God only in our family life and in church on Sundays. Over half our lives were out of bounds for God!

Now that we've recognized that our Good News is of a *transforming* God, that wall is coming down. The most promising invitation to Christians today may be the opportunity to get closer to our experience of work and to all that can mean to ourselves and many others.

Of course, we won't get anywhere with this opportunity unless we're realistic. For most people at present, their work is largely drudgery. And everyone's work has *some* negative aspects, like boredom, frustration, insecurity and staleness. *What are your main negative feelings about your job, with regard to*:

- the work you do
- how you're treated by your employer
- your relationships with your colleagues
- how your work ties into other parts of your life

What are your positive *feelings about those?*

Reflection

In 1988, 2000 people in Britain were asked *what they found the most important aspects of their work*. Their answers were:

1. Having control over what to do 50%
2. Using knowledge and experience to make decisions . 50%

3. Having a variety of things to do 39%
4. Amount you earn 35%
5. Being with and making friends 21%
6. Doing a job that you know people respect 19%

What they earned was important, for obvious reasons. But even more important for them was that central biblical insight: we were made to take "dominion" in a responsible, creative way. And, even in our individualistic times, the "community" aspect still has importance.

If you had been asked the same question, what would your answer have been?

How far do your positive and negative feelings about your present work arise from the presence or absence of the aspects that are important to you?

Response

> *Lord, I'm like you!*
> *The crown of my nature is my wanting to make things be*
> *to express my personality, my gifts, my knowledge*
> *in making a difference.*
> *Even my negative feelings can conspire towards this:*
> *they are signs that you give me, Lord, that such work may*
> *be against my nature.*
> *Help me use today's opportunities for making work*
> *more human,*
> *more creative and responsible,*
> *for myself and many others.*
>
> *Then we can shout with joy that we are like you,*
> *sharing in your happiness at making things be*
> *for a better life for all, in love.*

❧ Making Work Good ❧

Experience

Our work is meant to feel good, but at present often doesn't. There are no quick fixes. What, then, can help?

1. WE CAN GET IN CLOSE TOUCH WITH WHAT WE WANT FROM OUR WORK.

We all want some autonomy in our work. We want to put our own personal stamp on it. This gives it meaning for us.

It does that in different ways, depending on our personality. Many find being an expert the most meaningful part: for others, most of the meaning comes from caring about people and trying to humanize the atmosphere; for others, it's through being defenders of people or principles; for others, being innovators or self-developers.

Reflect on the goodness and the opportunities of your own way; and how they complement the ways of others you know well.

2. WE CAN HELP HUMANIZE.

Increasingly today, employers are realizing that humanizing work pays, and that failing to do so may well break the company. This clearly gives Christians a special opportunity to promote God's plan.

What are you already doing to make your workplace more human, and what more could you do? Some steps are obvious to all of us: ordinary acts of kindness; a caring eye for people in some worry or difficulty; encouraging friendliness, etc.

Then there are other steps that are likely to become common. They depend on the employer, but the work force can encourage them. Among them are:

- Trust more than control
- The work force having the right to criticize and make suggestions in regular meetings with the management
- Small interdisciplinary teams in factories, with workers

doing more than one operation on assembly lines
• Increase profit-sharing (1 1/2 million in UK in 1983)

What steps might be applicable to your kind of company?

Reflection

"We are entering a dynamic period when the economic imperative for a more competitive, more productive work force is leading us back to the kind of humanistic values of trust, freedom,
and respect for the individual. People are more productive if they
are treated with respect."

*God's transforming Rule is at present happening largely through
such factors as "the economic imperative," without much direct influ-
ence from Christians. What should be our response to that?*

Response

1. You are a member of your local church *as the person you are*:
your gifts, your needs, and the work you do (a large part of your
life!). Could the work-dimension of the members figure more
largely in the life and aims of the congregation?

2. You have your own particular approach to work: what can
give it meaning for you?

Accept that as one of God's greatest gifts to you, put into your
hands for you to use, enjoy and exploit, like the talents in Jesus'
story (Luke 19:12-27).

The People I Work With

❧ The Bond of Respect ❧

Experience

If you take some of your friends and ask them to tell you their experience of the people they work with, you'll probably get a varied batch of answers.

Some may talk of a real team spirit. At the other end of the scale, you'll hear strong complaints of things like injustice and sexual harassment.

The personal relationships we find in our workplace are likely to be a major part of our experience of our work. If they're bad, the everyday pressures of work are increased by such feelings as injustice, tense rivalry, and insecurity. If they're good, we have the sense of being in this together, of mutual respect and encouragement, and perhaps the pleasure of some close friendships.

Where, in that scale, comes your experience of the people you work with?

What are the chief influences that account for its present good, bad, or average quality?

Reflection

"Solidarity is a deep aspiration of the human spirit. It comes with effort and is maintained with effort."

In your workplace, what degree of solidarity do you favor? What kind of effort is necessary to create it and maintain it?

We won't have any degree of solidarity with our colleagues unless we at least respect them.

That's usually easy for people with whom we have a natural affinity or who have outstanding gifts. But it can be much more difficult with people of different approaches or habits to ourselves.

A very experienced psychotherapist once said to me: "There is no one I have *really* come to know whom I haven't liked"—and she must have treated, in her time, a few "difficult" people.

"Anyone who loves is a child of God" (1 John 4:7). They are like God. They are partners in God's work. Even if they have had no real opportunity to know Jesus Christ and his call.

How big is your responsibility, as a Christian, to respect and try to get to know your colleagues?

What are some of your main opportunities for doing that?

Response

Jesus, my friend, my brother and my Lord,
*   you were no stranger to mixed lots!*

Quite a mixture you had to cope with:
*   shocked rabbis,*
*   toll-collectors,*
*   notorious prostitutes of the town,*
*   your confused and sometimes scared disciples.*

You treated them all as good friends,
you wanted nothing but their good.

My workmates may be a bit "mixed,"
*   but not to that extent!*
Help me to be like you,
*   especially where that matters.*

❧ The Bond of Shared Experience ❧

Experience

As a Christian I try to respect, and if possible like, the people I work with. I try to treat them to some degree as friends.

But the other main bond that can unite us is, of course, the work itself. Whether we're enthusiastic, indifferent, or even cynical about the firm and its methods, we are, to some degree, sharing in the same enterprise.

This is a possible bond of shared experience, day in and day out, in some cases for years.

How far is that so, for you and for some of your colleagues?

Reflection

A recent poll has shown that most people believe in God. But that belief may be in some "ultimate expression," not in a very personal God working for us in our midst.

I can be a partner and sign of such a God by clearly living out my commitment to joining in God's work of transforming human life.

I must begin by sorting out in my own mind my actual work experience: my negative and positive feelings about it.

Some of these feelings may need deepening or correcting. They may be based on false information or misunderstanding.

To really get in touch with what my partnership with God means in practice, I need to go through two stages:

1. to bring to the surface my own feelings about my work, and to listen sympathetically to those of my colleagues.

2. then to look at my feelings and views as objectively as I can— if possible with a few others. In the light of the firm's economic situation, its actual policies and aims, what should be confirmed or changed? What could I/we do towards this? Whose interests,

other than our own, need to be considered: customers, shareholders, the local community, etc?

Christians have no monopoly on this—thank God! Our general approach may be the same as (or not as good as?) that of many of our non-Christian colleagues. What we have to contribute, through both those stages, is our conviction that *a loving God* is always at our side and that human transformation is his only aim. He is working through *all* of us, Christians and not.

The development of a common aim can be the bond which unites us.

Response

Colleagues at work often prefer to keep their relationship with each other quite casual. You may share that preference or habit; and of course you'll respect it in others.

But can we enter deeply into our own work experience unless we share our feelings and views about it with at least some others?

Can we help to humanize our work without that?

Consider whether you are called to help develop a greater solidarity among at least some of the work force for that purpose, so as to help yourself and others find the God working among us.

Your Boss

❧ Problems? ❧

Experience

The most obvious kind of leadership problem is the way the boss treats us. Perhaps he or she doesn't recognize my talents or my contribution: doesn't pay me enough; is insolent or aloof.

The other kind of leadership problem is usually related to the first. It's not just me that the boss deals with inadequately: it's also the task of leading this business enterprise.

The key to both problems often lies in the fact that the job description of a leader is undergoing great change. A successful leader has to adapt to that fact, and that's often not easy.

The results of a leader *not* doing that are often disastrous: "One-half of job-holders said they do not put effort into their job over and above what is required to hold onto it. A considerable gap exists between the number of hours people are paid for working and the number of hours spent in productive labor."

Does your boss treat you and your work adequately/inadequately? Is your boss adequate/inadequate as the leader of the company?

To what extent is there a relationship between the two answers?

Reflection

Why is the job description of a leader undergoing great change? It's because we've "suddenly woken up to the fact that organizations (are) made up of people." (Professor Charles Handy)

People give of their best if they have some autonomy, some control, some variety of things they do. We need to feel *trusted people*, not machines; we need to feel *we're going somewhere*; towards a vision that appeals to us.

Gone are the days when leading a work force was like pulling the levers of a large machine. Today's educated work force has rediscovered their human dignity. If the boss *doesn't* also do that, the gap between hours paid for and hours worked continues to be disastrous. If the boss *does* recognize it, then the company can do well.

"For Borg-Warner to succeed," said its 100 top managers in 1982, "we must operate in a climate of openness and trust."

The small print of that was expressed, in 1989, by the president of a large company: "Our company treats its 800 employees like responsible adults. Most of them—including factory workers—set their own working hours. All have access to the company's books. The vast majority vote on many corporate decisions."

Waking up to the fact that organizations are made up of people is patchy, and it takes many forms. But the present scarcity of skilled labor and other pressures are pushing all of us in this direction.

Response

> *Consider your colleagues at work,*
> *the people who will join in the next few years,*
> *your boss.*

You know that our one law is love. You want these people's good.

- what kind of work experience do you want for your colleagues and your boss?
- what kind of work-experience do you dream for the future?
- in the light of that "law," how important are these?

⁊ Towards Solutions ⁊

Experience

The Gospels show us Jesus' typical way of responding to people. He "noticed" them: entering into their actual situation. He did this with love and sympathy, and went on to act accordingly, even if that needed great courage.

The difficulties of being leader today may prompt us to respond to our boss in a similar way. Many of us have seen the relief of such a leader when he or she retires and the pressures are off. Two leaders told me, when they were just 50, that they were longing to retire.

But the importance of responding in Jesus' way to a leader comes also from another factor. The boss is *the leader*. But the function of *leadership* isn't only his or hers. Increasingly it is something in which we will have some share. By contributing to that development we make work more human and Christian for many.

"Old-fashioned management is easier than the new leadership. If the new organizations are going to succeed, our managers must think like leaders. Everyone with pretensions to be anyone must begin to think and act like a leader." (Professor Charles Handy)

Management is about pulling levers. *Leadership* is about responding to people as people and helping them "own" and achieve the goals of this enterprise.

In your firm, are you being encouraged to think and act like a leader? If so, what opportunities are being given? If not, what are the reasons?

Reflection

"You cannot ask people to behave like adults as homeowners, citizens, consumers, parents—and expect them to become docile children when they walk through a factory door."

It's because companies are increasingly realizing this that a firm like Apple Computers Inc. is looking for managers "who are coaches and team-builders and expanders, not controllers of people."

The question for us today isn't *whether* this trend will develop, but *how* it will develop, and *how extensively in our time.*

Response

Today we all need to be bridge builders between two kinds of leadership. That's difficult for all concerned. Somehow we've got to get it right.

What could you do:

- to "notice" the leader, as Jesus did: with love, sympathy, and appreciation: inviting him/her as leader into this process of bridge building?

- to encourage the (further?) development of leadership that responds to the humanity of the workforce and the objective reality of the company: e.g., by finding out what other companies do; promoting suitable kinds of discussion, at work and/or in your local church?

In such ways we will be exercising our own function and responsibility of leadership, for the good of our company, our fellow workers, and our successors.

My Faith

❧ What Difference Does It Make? ❧

Experience

You see a man with a microphone advancing towards you down the shopping mall in a purposeful manner. You move to avoid him, only to find yourself outflanked by a TV interviewer and the rest of the crew. Overcome by superior strategy, you agree to answer one question: "Why do you remain a Christian?"

If you agreed to answer, what would you say?

Reflection

What does being a Christian offer me?

Jesus gives me two things, closely intertwined: the assurance that God loves me; and my world usually tinged, and sometimes transfigured (in spite of appalling things), with joy and hope.

Scripture makes clear to me that no one knew God better than Jesus. He felt God's power in his gifts of healing; he felt his presence as "Father"; he saw God's transforming power, or "Kingly rule," breaking like great waves in the world and in the people around him.

God for him was not a set of concepts, but "harvest" or "feasting"; God was found in human life coming to a fuller and riper humanity, and in people sharing the joy and achievement of that.

My Christian faith puts me in touch with this kind of experience of life. It does so above all through the Scripture story. It does so also in the lives of some of the Christians I know and in my committing myself to share with the risen Jesus, alive in me through his resurrection power.

Like most people, I want life to be more human, and I'm prepared to work towards that. What my Christianity offers me is evidence for the rightness of that perspective and a glimpse of what it offers; and an invitation to find my full self by walking with Jesus.

EVERYWHERE I LOOK I KNOW THERE'S GROWTH: in pain or death I may not be able to see that. But the Christian story shows me that God is drawing everything towards rich harvest.

I KNOW THAT THE PERSONAL RULES: Fate often seems blind. A friend's marriage, career, or even life is destroyed by bad luck. Or everything seems aimless: there's no pattern or plan. I long for meaning in all this. I long for the tenderness, the strong encouragement, that I find in those I really know as persons.

Is a more massive proof of these two convictions conceivable than the Jesus story, both in Palestine and in those in whom he really lives?

Response

Lord, it's difficult for us to grasp it,
  we can't understand our luck,
You showed us what life is meant to be:
  its freedom, depth and warmth,
  its constant eruption into more lovely shapes and forms.
"All is yours," you said. "Take it. Make it be."
You showed this not in cold statement,
  but in a strong and gentle person: your Son.
With him we can take it, and make it be,
  bringing the happiness and hope that comes from meaning.

No soft option, Lord.
No walkover.
"Making things be" never was.
You have to give yourself to makes things grow, as your Son
  showed.
Let him be for me my way, my truth, and my life.

❧ All Shall Be Well ❧

Experience

As we recalled last week, we all have friends whose marriage broke up unexpectedly or who suddenly died. We know we can lose our job, or a limb, or a valued relationship, or our money. One moment there is sunshine; the next moment darkness.

How far is a feeling of insecurity part of your experience?

What worries you most?

Reflection

"There is absolutely no concept in the Old Testament with so central a significance for all the relationships of human life as God's 'integrity'."

God is completely dependable. His faithfulness and love will never let you down. "Those who know you, Lord, will trust you; you do not abandon anyone who comes to you" (Psalm 9:9).

It was this central conviction that gave rise, about 170 years before Christ, to the belief that there is life after death. That was a period, for the Jews, of horror and hopelessness. The God they had come to know *could not* let those win. This life *can't* be all there is. There would be "resurrection." The horizons of human hope had become immeasurably extended.

Jesus' "appearances" after his death convinced his shattered and dispersed followers that this immeasurably-extended kind of life was beginning now through Jesus. This Jesus was living in them. His quality of "resurrection" life was their life, too (cf Romans 8:10). The "new creation" had begun.

So "resurrection" wasn't just about life after death. It was about *the faithfulness of God being at the center of all* and about the full consequences of that being already partly experienced.

Few have suffered more than Paul. Few have known more acutely-felt failures. But even in the thick of these, joy wells up from his letters.

His confidence and joy arose from his one, central conviction that God has raised Jesus. He believed that "the resurrection of Jesus Christ is a declaration of God, through a particular man, of his eternal nature, his persistent purpose and his all-embracing promise."

Response

The Lord is a refuge for the oppressed,
*   a place of safety in times of trouble.*
Those who know you, Lord, will trust you;
*   you do not abandon anyone who comes to you.*
Protect me, O God; I trust in you for safety.
I say to the Lord, "You are my Lord;
*   all the good things I have come from you."*

I am always aware of the Lord's presence;
*   he is near, and nothing can shake me.*
And so I am thankful and glad
*   and I feel completely secure.*
You will show me the path that leads to life;
*   your presence fills me with joy*
*   and brings me pleasure for ever (Psalms 9 and 16).*

My Church

❧ What's My Church To *Me*? ❧

Experience

For some people their local church is just a building for worship where they are second-class citizens.

In Scripture, my local church is primarily a body of people who, each in their own "gift," equally share in the Spirit.

What's your local church to you?

Reflection

In sports, and in many jobs, it's great to work as a team. Each has their own "gift." Much of the time your "gift" is being affirmed and depended on, and you're doing the same for others. "You're OK. You're important," is the message coming through both *to* you and *from* you. You're sharing in helping people feel needed, act confidently, and grow. If it's sports, or enjoyable or challenging work, the experience can be exhilarating.

This fully human sharing is Scripture's requirement of the local church.

God called us to "fellowship with his Son," because we all equally share in his resurrection power, exercised in our "gifts" of service to others (1 Cor. 1:9; 12:4-7).

She's good at counselling; *he's* good at making people feel welcome; *she's* good at sensing how we might respond to a real need of the neighborhood; *that group's* good at involving members and proposing some strategies.

In spite of the huge pressures on people's time, all that, and much more, is present in every local church. The Good News of

God's coming to rule is *within* us. *HOW FAR WILL IT GET OUT AND BE HEARD?*

Response

1. If you had a billion dollars, you'd regard that as a great responsibility. Each of us has in fact a full share in Jesus' resurrection power.

Form a picture, in your own mind (or on paper) of:

a. how far this primary fact about a local church is appreciated in your local congregation.

b. further developments that could be considered.

2. Each of us is a full partner in our own special way.

Each person wants his/her life to "count": to be fruitful. "Remain in me," Jesus promised, "and you will bear much fruit" (John 15:5). It may be as a mother or father, or as helping to humanize my work, or by taking part in or supporting a service my local church offers for people's needs.

Take a different person you know well, each day this week:

• *try to appreciate better their charism and their fruitfulness, as where you can find God.*

• *ask yourself (and others?) how appreciation and support could grow.*

❧ What's My Church To *Them*? ❧

Experience

We ask ourselves: What's my church to *me*? or even to *us*? Obviously, both are excellent questions. But we're sometimes less apt to ask: What's my local church to *them*?

The point of a church is to "embody" Christ so as to make him realistically accessible to the people in that area.

What is your local church doing towards that?

How accessible to the people in the area are Christ's Good News about God's coming to us, and his compassionate and practical concern?

Reflection

JESUS proclaimed the Good News in the ways that were open to him.

There was just himself and a small group of perplexed and rather frightened men and women. He wasn't setting up an alternative worship group but summoning the whole nation. Apart from some synagogue preaching he used "unorthodox" measures, like preaching on the streets and inviting even social outcasts to dinner.

WE are in a different situation to Jesus. We are committed disciples and members of a sizeable body in a much more developed society. In some ways it is ready to hear about a "relevant" Christ.

"The credibility of today's church depends on how it relates to the world, affirming the goodness inherent in creation, denouncing those evil forces which set out to wreck the creative plan."

The new thing today is that this is becoming not just talk but is being done in many areas.

The church buildings cease to be just a private oasis, and become a campaign HQ. Fired by their partnership with Christ and with each other, the members go out to those whom Christ also loves.

Our "going out" can take many forms. Like Christ, we are free.

Like him we go out to liberate and enlighten, not to condemn. We go out to proclaim a resounding "yes" to the humanity of people.

Response

Should we become, as a 1985 Anglican report recommended, a "participating church":

- collaborating with the best expressions of local life?
- contributing to the transformation of life in the area?
- perhaps sharing our buildings and human skills with local groups?

What alternative or additional steps could your local church take to become more fully Good News?

Lord make me an instrument of your peace:
  where there is hatred, let me sow love;
  where there is injury, pardon;
  where there is doubt, faith;
  where there is despair, hope;
  where there is darkness, light;
  and where there is sadness, joy.

Our Worship

Enjoy

Experience

You can say "happy birthday" to your spouse because there'll be unpleasantness if you don't. You can say it because you feel it is the right thing to do. Or you can say it with all your heart: grateful, sometimes almost dazed, at your good luck at your partnership.

Which of these usually comes closest to your experience of worship?

When it is closest to the last type mentioned, what helps it to be like that?

Reflection

The earliest account of worship the Bible gives us is of a servant suddenly recognizing the hand of a wise and loving God in a sign that was given him when he was involved in a very important task (Genesis 24:27).

To begin with, he said no words. He bowed down. Through his whole person he expressed his wonder, awe, gratitude. Only *after* that did he use words. He "blessed" God for doing this. It was a great cry that said: "You're here: you're wonderful; my joy is my involvement in your story."

Such a cry we call a "eucharist." It isn't something that happens just in church services. It is the basic Christian mindset, as we've seen throughout this book. It is a "yes" with your whole person to sharing in God's involvement in human history. It's a cry of joy, of wonder, and commitment. Paul urges us to have that eucharist mindset "in all circumstances" (1 Thessalonians 5:18).

But we also need to develop and express that together. Hence the need for church services.

We are fellow members of Christ's body, so as to embody God's transforming power for our contemporaries in the history we share with them.

In our services we listen together to God's message to us, expressed in those deeds of power, and reflect together on our own role.

In a Eucharist prayer we can re-present the course of events in which God has been found in the past and is being found today as our shared response of joy and commitment to an ever richer discovery.

Response

All the churches are rediscovering, each in their own way, the Bible's view of worship.

In what ways do you (or could you) show support and appreciation for that re-discovery and help it go further, so that the other members and yourself:

- become more conscious, through the services, that being a Christian is to be "a participant in that course of events in which God through Jesus is present in a human fellowship (the Church) whose story is gospel"?

- to receive this Good News into our lives through listening to the Word of God?

- to express and deepen our commitment to this through the Eucharist prayer and Communion?

❧ Expressing Who We Are ❧

Experience

"The issue is not really one of liturgical forms, but of the sort of community, its direction, goals, vision, praxis, which is celebrating."

In what ways are those expressed, nourished and challenged in the worship of your local church?

"The Church is given the task of revealing the true God in the world." *In what ways does your church's worship help you and others know and love God and want to reveal him in the world?*

Apart from church services, how do you worship? Which ways do you find most helpful?

Reflection

God became known as the one for others. Freely, and with great love, he made a "covenant" with the whole human race (Genesis 15:18). Forever he would befriend them, protect them, bring them immeasurably good things. This covenant "represented, in all stages of Hebrew history, the dependable graciousness of God."

Jesus lived among us as the one for others. His only aim was to help people find "the treasure of great price" which he was experiencing in his Father's saving, healing power. Kindly, gentle, compassionate, he was as immovable as a rock in that work. He risked everything, lost everything, but persisted to the end in being "the one given for you" (Luke 22:19).

On his last evening he confirmed that true life is found through being for others by announcing God's "new covenant" (Luke 22:20).

In our worship we're not addressing a world "out there," but putting ourselves in intimate, enlivening touch with our life at its most true and real. We open ourselves to the holiness, the tenderness, the inexhaustible creativity of the God at the center of that life.

"This is your life," God always says. "Take it."

However falteringly, we do. In our marriage relationships, in our work, in our friendships and in our neighborhoods, we try to be for others.

Our worship is about our experience of that. It's where we express, nourish and challenge our accepting God's greatest gift. And in our Eucharists we commit ourselves to that in Jesus' covenant meal. We are his "body given for others." We will be the sign, for those around us, of "the dependable graciousness of God."

What is your own experience of being for others?

Response

"Our Eucharists are our creatively remembering that Christ's story is ours. Our eucharistic meal is thus deeply sacrificial in nature because in and through it the community is drawn into Christ's movement of self-gift." (Mary Grey)

How could you more deeply appreciate and use your opportunities to creatively remember that Christ's story is ours?

Are there ways in which the worship of your local church could better express, celebrate and nurture this community in its direction, goals, vision and praxis?

Death

❧ Death: How Bad? ❧

Experience

Andrew was dying of cancer, and had only a few weeks to live. His wife felt that he had some worry on his mind, and asked me to talk with him alone.

When I went into the bedroom, Andrew had some problems with his oxygen machine; but I was able to settle that. "Soon the machine won't be necessary," he said. The tone he said that in was the only indication of his feelings about the helplessness, the waste, the severing of so many ties of friendship and shared happiness. Andrew was only 49.

After a time I asked him whether he had any specific worries. "Yes," he said. "I've left Jane (his wife) too little money."

That wasn't the last time he showed his unselfishness. I was saying "good-bye," when another thought occurred to him: "I believe Dick (his son) has a guest for lunch today. Ask Jane to open a bottle of wine."

We've all met death, in various forms. Recall some of the things you have learned from these experiences.

Reflection

One thing we're likely to experience on such occasions is a sense of *helplessness and waste*. This person, with all that he or she means to me and others, will soon be no more. A theologian called death "the absurd arch-contradiction of existence."

Not surprisingly, for something so mysterious, we see it from several standpoints. As bodily people, we appreciate *a certain naturalness* about our dying. Also, would we in fact welcome an endless existence of one day after another? The fact that I will die means that *all the time I'm travelling towards my death*. This gives me a sense of the seriousness of life and of my need to give a direction and shape to what I am. If everything went on indefinitely, we might find this much more difficult.

In a sense we are dying all the time: trying to become the kind of person, the self, that we really want finally to be. I had seen Andrew doing that for many years, through more than his share of difficulties, but helped by his wife, his sons, and others.

How important is this dimension of death to you?

Response

If death is for me largely a help towards freely becoming the kind of self I want to be, is that the end of the matter? Or can we agree with this writer:

> Where an ultimate responsibility is assumed in obedience to a person's conscience,
>
> where ultimate selfless love and fidelity are given,
>
> where an ultimate selfless obedience to truth, regardless of self, is lived out, and so on,
>
> at this point there is really in our life something that is infinitely precious, that of itself has the right and reality not to perish, that is able to fill out an eternity, that actually deserves not merely to be rewarded by eternity but to claim this as its most authentic right, as its most intimate nature.

Even in our travelling towards dying, God has put into our nature this mystery and this promise.

PRAISE HIM.

❧ We Shall Not Die Alone ❧

Experience

With Jesus there came a new experience of life.

At the center of life, Jesus found the Father's liberating power. People were healed. People were brought back from isolation and hopelessness. The seeds of a new world order were beginning to grow.

The main point was his conviction that what was happening was *God's coming to power*. Behind this movement towards human wholeness and fulfillment was a loving Father who guided all.

Where would it lead? He did not know. But *all* was secure. The joy of a huge "harvest" was certain.

But *was* it so secure? Total failure, and a terrible death, increasingly loomed before him. Yet his last night he celebrated a Freedom meal with his friends. Wholeness *would* come.

The very reverse seemed to happen: a degraded shambles on a cross. All his followers dispersed.

The rest we know!

How full was Jesus' involvement in human life? You might consider, for example: his relationships with people, his concern for the sick and the rejected, his commitment to a new order, his parties and his stories, and the way he faced death.

Reflection

Jesus lived strongly as the self he wanted to be. He stood true to his conscience; he showed selfless love and fidelity. He filled out human life to an extraordinary degree.

The resurrection showed that "something that is infinitely precious has the right and reality not to perish." What we might *guess* from the very nature of human life *was found in practice to be true.*

101

Paul expresses his belief that that "infinitely precious reality" did not perish in the form of a huge cosmic scenario (in Philippians 2:6-11). It states that *because* Jesus plunged into the whole reality of human life, *therefore* God had made him the most alive and the most life-giving of all.

The whole of the New Testament is the story of *our sharing that aliveness* with Jesus. It's the story of our partnership with him. If we—like Andrew—aim at the self we really want to be, then "you are to think of yourselves as living in partnership with God, through Christ Jesus" (Romans 6:11).

Response

One day, Lord, I shall be like Andrew: dying.

I don't know how.

All I know is that you'll be there
    in that saving power you showed in Jesus'
    whole involvement in our human life,
    wanting for me the fulness of human life you showed
    in him.

Help me to reach out, at that moment, to your gift
    and say with all my heart,
"I want very much to leave this life and be with Christ,
    which is a far better thing" (Philippians 1:23).

Fullness of Life

Experience

Do you look forward to "heaven"?

When you're on a beach in fine weather, or enjoying a party with good friends, do you think: "This is fine, but I'd really prefer to be in heaven"?

In 1988, *Newsweek* found that 77% of Americans believe in heaven, but most believe it won't include the company of those close to them. The current picture is of a static, lonesome life, radically different from this one.

What is your picture of life after death?

On what is it based?

Reflection

Scripture offers us a picture of our future life closely related to this one:

1. *It's "bodily."* "God will also give life to your mortal bodies," says Paul (Rom. 8:11), just as God raised Jesus "bodily" from the dead.

My body is my capacity to be present to others. That's an essential part of being human. That capacity will remain, but will be transformed to a wider and deeper relatedness to others. Already we begin to sense the opportunities.

Scripture does not present us as consisting of two parts, body and soul. It's my *whole* self, including my body, that God cares about and will transform.

2. *It's like a feast.* Through the leisurely, relaxed dinner parties he gave, Jesus showed that the Father's coming in power through him has the characteristics of a party, with its shared enjoyment of human things. In his teaching, and in his last supper, he pictured the culmination of God's plan as a feast (Luke 14:15-24; 22:18,30). Imagine the laughter, the warmth, and the loving care shown in Jesus' parties.

3. *It's dynamic.* Jesus' resurrection was the evidence to his disciples that, through him, God was renewing all human life. Our resurrection is our full sharing in Jesus' fellowship with all humanity and in his supreme happiness of bringing it fulfillment. There are no spectators in the risen life. *All* are on the field.

4. *It's deeply human.* The fruit of Jesus' resurrection power (the Spirit) is a person who shows "love, joy, peace, patience, kindness, gentleness, humility, and self-control" (Gal. 5:22). In other words, it's where we've "become like God's Son" (Rom. 8:29).

Response

> *I am certain that neither death nor life,*
> *nothing in all creation*
> *will ever separate us from the love of God*
> *which is ours through Christ Jesus our Lord (Rom. 8:38-39).*

> *Lord,*
> *let me live in your love*
> *and let me live your love*
> *forever.*

❧ What Will It *Feel* Like? ❧

Experience

Most years I send out Christmas cards. Some are to people who live quite near me. But some are to loved friends in distant countries whom I seldom see.

Many of these people I'd love to be with very often. But even the friends who live quite near I may not see for months. And even with those I see regularly and think I know well, I often eventually find that I have been blind to some of their deepest concerns and finest qualities.

Even if I were able to enjoy fully all my friends, millions of people, and most of the world's cultures, would remain a closed book. There is a huge richness in human life from which I am at present barred. And, as one who travels for his job, I have more access to them than many others do.

Do you sometimes feel that you are at present barred from much of the richness of human experience? And what about the poor?

Is this what God wants for us?

Reflection

Take a four-year-old round a sophisticated art exhibition. Or try to convey to him or her what it's like to be married. With skill, you can make a start. But anything like a full appreciation will be impossible until the child lives on a more adult "frequency."

Things like sending out Christmas cards can remind us that even with telephones, modern travel, and the rest, we still live on a very limited human frequency. "The range of the real world must transcend quantitatively and qualitatively, by inconceivable dimensions, the horizon of knowledge available to us at the present level of development."

It's not just our present knowledge and experience that is limited but also our possession of it. We do have moments of success or even ecstasy, but usually they are in the future, or in the past, and they exist only briefly in our actual experience.

The point of Jesus, and now of us his body, is to give our contemporaries a glimpse, even in this limited frequency, of the range and richness of the real world which God has made ours.

Now that we've tried to become more involved in this, through our praying, we can better imagine what it would be like:

• If we really knew and entered deeply into the lives of others and delighted in our interdependence and fellowship;

• if we shared the achievement and joy of this with Jesus;

• if we recognized in this the perfect life of God: "an endlessly dynamic movement of experience, ecstasy, exploration and activity";

• if we knew that "all is ours" and that all of us are at home;

• if we had endless possibilities in this of deep sharing.

Response

"The glory of God is a man or woman fully alive" (Irenaeus).

*You have done many things for us, O Lord our God,
    there is no one like you.*

*You have made many wonderful plans for us.
I could never speak of them all—
    their number is so great (Psalm 40:5).*